ABORTION AND DIVORCE
IN WESTERN LAW

The 1986 Julius Rosenthal Foundation Lectures
Northwestern University Law School

ABORTION AND DIVORCE
IN WESTERN LAW

MARY ANN GLENDON

HARVARD UNIVERSITY PRESS
CAMBRIDGE, MASSACHUSETTS
AND LONDON, ENGLAND
1987

Library of Congress Cataloging-in-Publication Data
Glendon, Mary Ann, 1938–
    Abortion and divorce in Western law.

    (Rosenthal lectures; 1986)
    Bibliography: p.
    Includes index.
    1. Abortion—Law and legislation—United States.
2. Divorce—Law and legislation—United States.   3. Abortion—Law and legislation—Europe.   4. Divorce—Law and
legislation—Europe.   I. Title.   II. Series.
KF5181.G58   1987   346.01′66   87-7534
                         342.6166
ISBN 0-674-00160-5 (alk. paper)

For Joseph F. Flanagan

CONTENTS

ABORTION AND DIVORCE
IN WESTERN LAW

INTRODUCTION

This book concerns two subjects that have been discussed extensively, some might even say excessively, in both scholarly and popular literature: abortion and divorce. It is reasonable, therefore, to wonder what comparative legal analysis could possibly be expected to add to the thorough airing these topics have had in recent years. A preliminary response of the sort that comparatists like to give would be that comparative lawyers are drawn to the study of problems that their own legal systems do not handle very well. Indeed, it may be that the most interesting subjects for comparison are those problems that are not only unresolved but perhaps not susceptible of resolution in any definitive sense. When comparatists devote their attention to this kind of issue, it is generally not with the idea that they will find in some foreign land a "solution" which, like a new electrical appliance, can be fitted with an adapter and plugged into the system back home. What they are usually looking for is, at a minimum, a deepened understanding of the problem and, if they are lucky, a source of inspiration. Since controlled experimentation in law is hardly ever possible, legal scholars often use comparative law, just as they sometimes consult history, to see how legal systems of the past or present have dealt with problems similar to ours. The hope is that history and comparison will give us insight into our own situation and that they may occasionally help us to find, as John P. Dawson once put it, "our own paths through the forest."[1]

The subjects examined here have worn such grooves in our thinking that it is only through comparison that we become aware, first of a puzzle, and then of several matters that seem to require explanation. The puzzle here is this: the United States, while participating generally in the overall trends that have marked the recent transformation of Western family law, often occupies an extreme end of the spectrum when cross-national comparisons are made on specific issues. This is the case with its legal treatment of abortion, of certain aspects of divorce, and of those forms of dependency which are connected with pregnancy, marriage, and child raising.

The results of comparative surveys of abortion and divorce law in twenty countries are reported in Chapters 1 and 2 respectively, with special attention to the related topic of the legal treatment of dependency. When American abortion law is viewed in comparative perspective, it presents several unique features. Not only do we have less regulation of abortion in the interest of the fetus than any other Western nation, but we provide less public support for maternity and child raising. And, to a greater extent than in any other country, our courts have shut down the legislative process of bargaining, education, and persuasion on the abortion issue. Divorce law in the United States is also distinctive in a number of ways. Divorce is as readily available in most American states as it is anywhere, but we have been less diligent than most other countries in seeking to mitigate the economic casualties of divorce through public assistance or enforcement of private support obligations.

In the third chapter I consider whether the techniques of comparative law, having been directed toward several vexing problems in contemporary American law and having discovered that the legal approaches of the United States to these problems are anomalous, can contribute anything toward explaining the anomalies or resolving the problems. Since so much of the distinctiveness of American law in the areas examined here seems to have been unintended, the question arises whether there are special factors that might have facilitated the development here of these unusual approaches to divorce, abortion, and dependency. Why, in the United States more than elsewhere, is the abortion debate dominated by talk of "rights"? Why did the term "no fault divorce" arise and take hold in the context of American divorce law reform? I attempt to show in Chapter 3 that the roots of these American differences can be traced in part to phenomena in the realm of ideas—to a way of thinking about law that gained greater predominance in the Anglo-American world than elsewhere, and to different types of linkages that were made between law and political theory in the common law and civil law systems. My intent is not to minimize the role of other cultural factors, but to call attention to the fact that political and legal ideas have played no small part in forming the distinctively American way of imagining the individual in his or her relationships to others in the family and larger communities.

One of the aims of this book is to make a case for wider attention to and greater use of comparative legal analysis, by showing how awareness of foreign experiences can illuminate our own situation and contribute in a modest way to our own law reform efforts. With this in mind, and because some of the techniques of legal comparison that I have used are not conventional ones, a short preliminary discourse on comparative method is in order. According to the late Sir Otto Kahn-Freund, comparative law is merely "the common name for a variety of methods of looking at law."[2] Because many of these methods were developed in the late nineteenth century, it should not be surprising that, like the legal science of which they were a part, they have not proved fully adequate to the analysis of contemporary legal problems. Modern comparative law took shape as a discipline when French and German scholars began the systematic study of other legal systems in connection with the extraordinary flurry of legislative activity that took place in those countries in the last decades of the nineteenth century.[3] The conceptual apparatus developed in the *belle époque* of comparative law was characteristic of the normal legal science of that period. It concentrated on formal rules, institutions, and procedures; it took the primacy of private law for granted, largely ignoring public law; and its sources-of-law theory assumed the centrality of case law in the Anglo-American systems and of civil codes in the Romano-Germanic systems.

To these early comparatists, differences among the Western legal systems seemed greater than they do to us. The national codifications on the Continent had accentuated the sense of the distinctiveness of each country's law, and seemingly had marked the disintegration of that common European legal culture that was a sturdy hybrid of received Roman law, Germanic customs, canon law, and the law merchant. In fact, to a great extent the continental and Anglo-American countries still shared and were influenced by a common Western legal inheritance. But appreciation of this fact was not restored until comparative methodology, along with legal theory in general, became more refined in the early twentieth century. Between the two world wars, comparatists such as Ernst Rabel in Germany and Edouard Lambert in France began to insist on the importance of inquiring into how legal rules and institutions actually operate in practice, and of seeing them in their full social and economic context. These scholars were to their immediate predecessors as comparative physiologists are to comparative anatomists—more concerned with systems and functions than with structures and rules. Theirs was a period of discovery of essential similarities behind formal differences. A favorite kind of demonstration was to show that, despite very different substantive rules regarding, say, contracts, there was a high degree of similarity of outcomes in contracts cases presenting similar facts. Today, with hindsight, it is easy for us to perceive an even deeper similarity among turn-of-the-century Western legal systems. We now recognize that behind their divergent rules, methods, and institutions, the French, German, English, and American legal systems of that time were to a great extent infused with similar animating principles protecting and promoting private property, freedom of contract, and the patriarchal family.

The developing field of social theory found yet another role for comparative law in the early twentieth century. This was the use of comparisons by Durkheim, Pareto, Weber, and others to illuminate the complex interactions among law, behavior, and ideas, and to explore the connections between legal and social change. The use of comparative law as a heuristic device was brought to its highest form in the legal sociology of Max Weber.

To some extent, all of the foregoing methods of looking at law have been employed in the studies of abortion and divorce law presented here, but the inquiry here has also been influenced by a different conception of comparative law, which is both older and newer. For this, Plato's *Laws* is the foundational text. The *Laws* is the last, longest, and most political of Plato's dialogues. It probably is, or should be, of more interest to legal scholars than to philosophers, who generally consider it to be far from Plato's greatest work. But its manifest good will toward the study of foreign law warms the heart of the comparatist even as it draws us into dialogue with the text. The text, among other things, suggests a way of looking at law which comparatists often neglect.

The protagonist of the *Laws* is a traveler far from his native city, an old man who doesn't even have a name. Plato calls him the Athenian Stranger. In some ways he reminds us of the Socrates of the earlier dialogues, but he is less charming and more pious, less elegant in diction and more urgent in purpose. It may be that this is as close as we get to hearing the voice of Plato himself,[4] but if so, it is the Plato who was approaching the end of his own journey through the world.

The dialogue takes place between the Athenian and two other elderly pilgrims, a Cretan and a Spartan, whom he has encountered on the road from Knossos to the cave and temple of Zeus on the island of Crete. Both Crete and Sparta were renowned in the ancient world for their laws, and the shrine which is the travelers' destination commemorates the divine origin of the laws of Crete. At first it seems that the Athenian may have come to Crete to learn about these laws, for the dialogue opens with his blunt question to the others: "Is it a god or some human being, strangers, who is given the credit for laying down your laws?"[5] When Kleinias the Cretan and Megillos the Spartan reply, somewhat equivocally, that their lawgivers were indeed gods,[6] the Athenian Stranger proposes that it might be pleasant to beguile the time on their journey with conversation about the government and laws of Crete and Sparta. Soon we learn that Kleinias has just been appointed to a commission charged with the duty of establishing a new Cretan colony, complete with a constitution and laws. He has been told that if he and his colleagues should discover some laws from elsewhere that appear to be better than Cretan laws, they are not to worry about their being foreign. It would thus be helpful to him,

Kleinias suggests, if the three travelers could spend the day founding a city in speech as they stroll and rest on the way to their common destination.[7]

This request appears to be what the Stranger was waiting for all along.[8] No longer the idly curious student of foreign institutions, he now dominates the ensuing discussion, which ranges over the great perennial questions of the purpose of law; the relations between law and custom, law and power, law and justice, law and what we would today call a particular culture, courts and legislatures; and the extent to which the law should attempt to regulate the private lives of citizens. Along the way no important political or moral principle is left unexamined.[9] Family law, starting with marriage and the upbringing of children, is a central topic.

At the end of the day, the Stranger reminds his companions that their aim has been to devise laws for a real city and not some ideal republic;[10] consequently, the law making process will have to be an ongoing one. Since the city must constantly be re-examining and revising its laws, its Guardians would do well, he advises, to send out mature citizens to study especially good laws elsewhere, and to seek assistance from wise persons wherever they may be found, even in ill-ordered cities. And, finally, he says that the city should always be willing to receive strangers of either sex who have something important to teach or who have come with a serious desire to learn.[11] How can the comparatist not be enchanted? True, we suspect that for Plato, as for Montesquieu and Tocqueville, discourse about foreign systems is in part just a safe and convenient literary device for raising certain issues about politics and law at home. Even so, we are won over. But won over to what?

From the beginning to the end of the *Laws,* no matter what legal subject is raised, it is education which always comes to the fore. The ultimate concern here, as in *The Republic,* is not so much with the right laws for the state, but with the right education for citizenship.[12] The Athenian Stranger continually brings the discussion around to the classical idea that the aim of law is to lead the citizens toward virtue, to make them noble and wise. The Stranger stresses, further, that the lawgiver has not only force but also persuasion at his disposal as a means to accomplish this aim. He drives the latter point home by comparing the legislator who simply issues commands to a certain kind of doctor whom he calls the slave doctor. The slave doctor, a slave himself, has learned what he knows of medicine by working as the servant of a doctor. His manner of practicing his profession is to make a hurried visit, to order whatever remedy experience suggests, and then to rush off to the next patient. By contrast, the freeman's doctor begins by getting to know the patient and his family. He inquires far back into the nature of the disorder, and when he has got as much information as possible, he then begins instructing the patient with the aim of restoring his health by persuading him into compliance. This doctor gives his prescriptions only after he has won the patient's understanding and cooperation.

As for the law maker, the Athenian Stranger asks, should he merely issue a set of commands and prohibitions, add the threat of a penalty, and then go on to another law, offering never a word of advice or encouragement to those for whom he is legislating?[13] This kind of law may be fit for slaves, he suggests, but surely a legislator for free men should try to devise his laws so as to create good will in the persons addressed and make them ready to receive intelligently the command that follows.[14]

I bring up these old ideas about law for two reasons. First, they are essential to understanding some of the most important differences between the approaches of Anglo-American and continental European law to the specific problems this book examines. In addition, they seem to be closely connected to some of the most interesting contemporary American thinking about law. In England and the United States the view that law is no more or less than a command backed up by organized coercion has been widely accepted. The idea that law might be educational, either in purpose or technique, is not popular among us.[15] But on the European continent, older ideas about law somehow survived the demolition of classical political theory and have persisted, at least as undercurrents, into the modern age.[16] The rhetorical method of law making appears not only in the great continental codifications, but also, here and there, in all sorts of contemporary European legislation. It is most especially evident in continental family law.

In England and the United States, where prevailing legal theory tends to deny or downplay any pedagogical aim of law, legislation tends to be in the form of the prescriptions of the slave doctor. But recently a few American scholars have begun to talk about looking at law in a way that would not have sounded entirely strange to Plato. James Boyd White suggests, for example, that "law is most usefully seen not . . . as a system of rules, but as a branch of rhetoric, . . . as the central art by which community and culture are established, maintained and transformed."[17] And from another branch of the human sciences has come a related invitation or challenge directed specifically to comparatists. In his Storrs lectures at Yale Law School, the anthropologist Clifford Geertz advised comparative lawyers that they would learn and contribute more if they focused on the fact that law is not just an ingenious collection of devices to avoid or adjust disputes and to advance this or that interest, but also a way that a society makes sense of things. It is "part of a distinctive manner of imagining the real."[18] From this perspective, the interesting comparisons among legal systems should lie, first, in their manner of characterizing factual situations so that rules can be applied to them, and second, in how they conceive of the legal norms themselves. It is to be expected that legal systems compared in this manner will differ in the "stories they tell," the "symbols they deploy," and the "visions they project."[19] The comparatist's task thus becomes a venture into cultural hermeneutics.

The approaches advocated by Geertz and White seem especially promising for the comparative analysis of the subjects treated here. Whether meant to or not, law, in addition to all the other things it does, tells stories about the culture that helped to shape it and which it in turn helps to shape: stories about who we are, where we came from, and where we are going. The stories that are going forward at a given time in a legal system seem to have a powerful influence not only on how legal norms are invented and applied within that system, but on how facts are perceived and translated into the language and concepts of the law. Indeed, it may be that law affects our lives at least as much by these stories as it does by the specific rules, standards, institutions, and procedures of which it is composed. Thus it is not an unworthy task for scholars to ask how law interprets the world around it, what analogies and images it employs, what segments of history and what aspects of human experience it treats as relevant.

Two aspects in particular of the rhetorical activity of law will receive special attention in the chapters that follow—the interpretive and the constitutive. Law is interpretive when it is engaged in converting social facts into legal data and systematically summarizing them in legal language. All lawyers are aware that before legal norms can be devised or applied, those facts that are to be treated as legally relevant must be selected out from a complex manifold of words, deeds, and events. In this process much is disregarded, and what is retained is presented in a stylized, pared-down version. Geertz has aptly pointed out that, "Whatever law is after, it is not the whole story."[20] This problem is, of course, not confined to law. In every form of discourse, the choice of a word is an endowment of meaning, an act of symbolic formulation. In the present work, some of the most interesting differences that emerge among legal systems concern the divergent ways in which social data are imaginatively reconstructed as legal facts and concepts.

The interpretive aspects of law are closely related to its constitutive qualities. Law is constitutive when legal language and legal concepts begin to affect ordinary language and to influence the manner in which we perceive reality. As White has put it, law is "an element in the perpetual remaking of the language and the culture that determines . . . who we are" as individuals and as a society.[21] This way of looking at law suggests a number of questions that I wish to pursue here, in the context of divorce and abortion law as well as of the legal treatment of economic dependency related to child raising. What stories are being told in these bodies of law at the present time? How do these stories affect what issues are raised and treated as important and which are excluded from discussion or perhaps even obscured from view? Is there a distinctively American story? What sorts of meaning is family law creating and what sort of society is it helping to constitute?[22]

ONE

ABORTION LAW

To one interested in comparative family law, Geertz's invitation to view law as part of a distinctive way of imagining the real is especially appealing. Much of family law is no more—and no less—than the symbolic expression of certain cultural ideals. The older continental European civil codes told wives that they should obey their husbands, and children of all ages that they should honor and respect their parents.[1] Today, modernized versions of the same codes tell husbands and wives that they are equal partners in running a household,[2] and a recent Swedish law tells parents that they should not punish by spanking or otherwise humiliating their children.[3] Probably no other area of law is so replete with legal norms that communicate ideas about proper behavior but that have no direct sanctions.

THE ABORTION REVOLUTION

To a great extent, modern Western family law systems appear to imagine reality in similar ways.[4] But major differences do appear in some areas, both in the way the law articulates the underlying problems and in the way in which rules have been devised to deal with the problems once they have been characterized. One of these areas is that of abortion, which Gilbert Steiner has called "the most intractable and most prominent of family policy issues."[5] It seems a particularly suitable area in which to try out Geertz's suggested approach, because no aspect of Western law affecting family life has been more controversial, and because the way that

American law in particular has imagined the situation is so distinctive. Thus I propose to explore in this chapter some of the interpretive and constitutive aspects of abortion regulation in a group of twenty countries that includes the United States, Canada, and eighteen West European countries (Austria, Belgium, Denmark, England, Finland, France, West Germany, Greece, Iceland, Ireland, Italy, Luxembourg, the Netherlands, Norway, Portugal, Spain, Sweden, and Switzerland).

The first striking finding of a comparative survey of abortion regulation is that fundamental change has occurred in this area all over the Western world in a relatively short period of time. Within less than two decades all but three of these twenty nations abandoned strict abortion laws—introduced for the most part in the nineteenth century[6]—in favor of a more permissive stance.[7] Between 1967, when England and three American states (California, Colorado, and North Carolina) relaxed their legal restrictions on abortion, and 1985, when Spain became the most recent country to do so, the legal approach to the question of when and under what conditions voluntary termination of pregnancy should be permitted changed widely, rapidly, and radically. Furthermore, of the three countries that did *not* significantly change their abortion laws in this period (Belgium, Ireland, and Switzerland), one (Switzerland) had already liberalized its strict statute in the 1940s.

How can one account for this sudden wave of change affecting countries with so many political, cultural, and religious differences from each other? There were, to be sure, as John Noonan has observed, certain "background" factors operating in the 1960s.[8] The appearance of the long-awaited birth control pill and the mood of the times had spurred re-examination of traditional attitudes toward sexuality and sex roles. World population growth had become a prominent concern of several organizations at both national and international levels. More specific factors also became influential. Under the strict abortion laws that became standard in the late nineteenth century, abortions were permitted where necessary to save the life of a pregnant woman. At the time these laws were adopted, there were in fact many indications for life-saving abortions, such as tuberculosis, cardiovascular and renal disease, and the so-called pernicious vomiting of pregnancy.[9]

11

By the 1960s, however, advances in medicine meant that it was only a rare case where the pregnant woman's life could be said to be at stake. Fewer and fewer abortions were being performed to preserve the woman's life or even physical health. The numbers revealed how many had always been and were still being performed for other reasons. With its cover story gone, the medical profession began to be concerned about protecting its legal position and to become an active and powerful force for liberalization.

A *cause célèbre* is always useful to law reformers, and the abortion reform movement found one in the thalidomide scandal of the 1960s. This drug, which has a high potential for causing severe deformities in children of women who take it during pregnancy, was never approved for sale in the United States, but it appeared on the market in several other countries. It helped to bring the abortion issue before the American public in a vivid way in the case of a woman named Sherri Finkbine who, while pregnant, had taken some thalidomide tablets obtained abroad. When Mrs. Finkbine learned of the dangers associated with the drug, she tried unsuccessfully in New York and Arizona to have an abortion under medical supervision, even going to the length of asking an Arizona court for a declaratory judgment that her doctors could terminate her pregnancy without violating Arizona law.[10] Eventually, Mrs. Finkbine had an abortion in Sweden. The fetus turned out to have been affected by the drug. By then, articles on her plight had been prominently featured in the *New York Times*. Her story, as well as those of numerous "thalidomide babies" born in England, Belgium, and West Germany, was presented with sympathy in women's magazines and in sensational fashion in tabloids. They dramatized one aspect of the abortion issue for a wide cross-section of the public.

Once the English Abortion Act of 1967 was adopted, it too contributed to the momentum for abortion law reform. Discussions and studies leading up to the adoption of the English statute had resulted in a heightened level of awareness, both in and outside England, of the problem of illegal abortion and the phenomenon of "abortion tourism." After the new statute went into effect, England itself began to attract a considerable number of abortion-seeking travelers. Observers in other countries, some with satisfaction and some with dismay, realized that what had happened in England was possible elsewhere. Finally, although abortion law reform was not at first defined by its proponents as a women's issue, the rise of groups dedicated to improving the position of women gave great impetus to the movement for easier access to abortion in the 1970s and thereafter.[11]

At present, the wave of fundamental change in abortion law appears to have crested and subsided. Thus, this seems an appropriate moment to examine these new abortion laws comparatively, to see to what extent they represent different ways of characterizing the factual situations they purport to govern and of imagining the principles, standards, and rules that are to be applied to these situations. My focus will therefore be mainly on the basic regulation of the conditions under which abortion is permitted. But from time to time it will be necessary to refer also to what one might call bureaucratic abortion law, such as regulation of funding for abortions, as well as for social welfare programs designed to help pregnant women continue with a pregnancy to term. This type of law, too, has both an interpretive and a constitutive function.

ABORTION REGULATION IN TWENTY COUNTRIES

Of the twenty countries whose law was surveyed for the present study, only two—Belgium and Ireland—have blanket prohibitions against abortion in their criminal law, subject to the defense of necessity.[12] (See Table 1.) Twelve countries take a middle position, disapproving of abortion in principle, but permitting it under some circumstances for what the legislature has deemed to be good cause.[13] The remaining six countries, including the United States, expressly permit elective abortion, at least in the early stages of pregnancy.[14] In the twelve countries that occupy the middle band of this spectrum, abortion is permitted on a variety of grounds.[15] In practice, in most of these middle-range countries it now seems quite easy for a woman legally to terminate an unwanted pregnancy in the first trimester. There can, of course, be a significant discrepancy between a country's legal norms regarding abortion and the practice of abortion it tolerates. For example,

13

Table 1. Legal Regulation of Abortion in Twenty Countries (with dates of major change in approach)

Abortion Illegal (defense of necessity)	Abortion for Cause		Elective Abortion	
	Hard grounds only[a]	Soft grounds in early pregnancy[b]	Elective in early pregnancy; strictly regulated thereafter	Elective until viability; regulation thereafter permitted but not required[c]
Belgium	Canada (1969)	England (1967)	Austria (1974)	U.S.A. (1973)
Ireland	Portugal (1984)	Finland (1970)	Denmark (1973)	
	Spain (1985)	France (1975)	Greece (1978, 1986)	
	Switzerland (1942)	West Germany (1976)	Norway (1975, 1978)	
		Iceland (1975)	Sweden (1974)	
		Italy (1978)		
		Luxembourg (1978)		
		Netherlands (1981)		

[a] The so-called hard grounds typically involve serious danger to the pregnant woman's health, likelihood of serious disease or defect in the fetus, or situations where the pregnancy resulted from rape or incest.
[b] The so-called soft grounds typically permit abortion under a variety of circumstances which pose exceptional hardship for the pregnant woman.
[c] Under *Roe v. Wade*, reasonable regulation to protect maternal health is permitted after the end of the first trimester, but the Supreme Court has taken a strict view of what is to be considered reasonable.

legal abortions are relatively easy to obtain in Belgium despite the apparent severity of the law there, while they are more difficult to obtain in some regions of West Germany than its relatively lenient federal statute would lead one to suppose.

The main purpose of the inquiry here, however, is not to ascertain how easy or difficult it is for a pregnant woman to obtain a legal abortion. It is rather to examine the messages about such important matters as life and liberty, individual autonomy and dependency, that are being communicated both expressly and implicitly by abortion regulation. For this purpose we have to look more closely at some of these systems of regulation. The abortion law of France, a compromise statute enacted and held constitutional in 1975, is particularly instructive in this respect. France is sometimes classified as an abortion-on-demand jurisdiction, but, as the following discussion indicates, it is more correct to group it with the countries which permit abortion only for a reason.

The Middle Way

In France since 1975 abortion has been available, up to the end of the tenth week of pregnancy, to any woman "whose condition places her in a situation of distress."[16] "Distress" is not defined, and the statute makes the woman herself the sole judge of whether she is in it.[17] No doctor or bureaucrat need certify anything regarding her state. Thus if all one is interested in is how easily an abortion can be obtained, it would be correct to say that in fact there is abortion on demand in France in the first ten weeks of pregnancy. But so far as the way abortion law imagines reality is concerned, there is a considerable difference between saying that the decision whether or not to abort is up to the woman, and saying that the state recognizes this option only in the case of women who are "in distress." Like the provision of the French Civil Code which still insists that spouses owe each other fidelity,[18] the "distress" requirement may have no direct sanction, and many people may not take it seriously, but it does communicate a message which *may* enter, along with other social forces, into the way in which French men and women think—and teach their children and each other—about how one should conduct one's life.

Like the 1970 change in the French code from the provision that said "The husband is the head of the family" to one that announced the equality of the spouses,[19] several parts of the 1975 statute which liberalized French abortion law are clearly meant to serve a symbolic and hortatory function. The first article of the 1975 law characterizes the factual situation upon which the law operates as involving human life, and sets forth the general principles that are to guide the interpretation of the new legislation: "The law guarantees the respect of every human being from the commencement of life. There shall be no derogation from this principle except in cases of necessity and under the conditions laid down by this law."[20]

In 1979 the following language was added to this section, indicating that the state was to take an active part in promoting respect for life, not just a negative role by restricting abortions: "The teaching of this principle and its consequences, the provision of information on the problems of life and of national and international demography, education towards responsibility, the acceptance of the child in society, and family-oriented policy are national obligations."[21]

Another statement of principle is set forth in a later section of the law: "The voluntary termination of pregnancy must under no circumstances constitute a means of birth control. To this end, the government shall take all the measures necessary to promote information on birth control on as wide a scale as possible."[22]

After affirming the principle of respect for human life, the 1975 law then specifies the circumstances under which it will countenance derogation from that principle, calling these circumstances cases of "necessity."[23] The law, imitating life in this respect, is not strictly logical in carrying out its basic principles. The first case of "necessity" it acknowledges is when, prior to the end of the tenth week of pregnancy, a woman finds herself in "distress" as a result of being pregnant.[24] But while making abortion available in this case, the statute mandates several procedures designed to make the pregnant woman aware of, and able to choose, alternatives to abortion. First, the physician who receives the woman's initial request for termination of her pregnancy must furnish her with a brochure (supplied by the government) informing her that the law limits abortion to cases of distress.[25] (There are no sanctions against the woman who pretends to be in distress. The idea seems to be simply to try to make sure everyone knows that abortion is considered to be a serious matter.) The brochure must contain information about the public benefits and programs that are guaranteed to mothers and children, and about the possibilities of adoption, as well as provide a list of organizations capable of giving assistance.[26] Second, the pregnant woman is required to have a private interview, if possible with her partner, with a government-approved counseling service which, in principle, is not to be located in any facility where abortions are performed.[27] This consultation, according to the statute, is supposed to furnish the woman with assistance and advice, "especially with a view toward enabling her to keep her child."[28] Third, at least one week must elapse from the time of her initial request for an abortion, and at least two days from the time of the mandatory consultation, before the abortion can be performed.[29] The waiting periods need not be observed if, in the physician's judgment, there is an emergency situation, or if they would cause the ten-week period to be exceeded.[30]

After ten weeks the law in France permits only "therapeutic" abortions. In these cases, two physicians must certify that the "continuation of the pregnancy is seriously endangering the woman's health or that there is a strong possibility that the unborn child is suffering from a particularly serious disease or condition considered incurable at the time of diagnosis."[31] To avoid bringing "abortion mills" into existence, the law provides that all abortions must be performed by physicians in approved facilities, and that the annual number of abortions in such establishments may not exceed 25 percent of all surgical and obstetrical operations carried out there.[32] At present, in France, the state pays 70 percent of the cost of nontherapeutic abortions and the entire cost of those that are medically necessary.[33]

Immediately upon its passage and before promulgation, the seventy-seven legislators who had opposed the 1975 law brought it to the French Constitutional Council for review, on grounds that it violated constitutional guarantees of human rights and protection of the health of children.[34] The council, which, unlike the United States Supreme Court, has rarely been inclined to differ with the parliamentary majority on a highly controversial question, upheld the law in a very short opinion. It began by noting that the Constitution "does not confer upon the Constitutional Council a general power of evaluation and decision identical with that of the Parliament, but gives it jurisdiction only to rule on the conformity to the Constitution of the laws submitted for its scrutiny."[35] The council ruled that the law did not violate any constitutional texts. The principle of respect for life was, in the council's view, satisfied by the fact that the statute permitted abortion only in case of necessity and under the conditions provided by law.

It would be easy to adopt a cynical attitude toward the French legislation. It could fairly be described as a political compromise which not only permits but funds abortion on the softest of soft grounds, while handing a bouquet of platitudes about human life to those whose position the legislature has rejected. But from another point of view it seems as though the French law makers had taken to heart Montesquieu's advice that "The spirit of a legislator ought to be that of moderation, political good . . . lying always between two extremes."[36] Let us remember that France, like the United States, was deeply and bitterly divided on the abortion question.[37] The legislation that was adopted there may be a melange of elements pleasing to few and offensive to many, yet, since its passage, France has had no continuing high-level turmoil on the issue of abortion. The 1975 law, which was to expire by its own terms after five years, was re-enacted without any such sunset clause in 1979 with a few minor changes in its provisions.

At a minimum, one could say for the present French abortion legislation that it is a humane, democratic compromise. But one could, I think, say more. Evidence that a great tradition of legislative drafting is still alive in France, the combination of its elements is greater than the sum of the parts. The legislation as a whole is pervaded by compassion for pregnant women, by concern for fetal life, and by expression of the commitment of society as a whole to help minimize occasions for tragic choices between them. This commitment is carried out by provision of birth control assistance, and by comparatively generous financial support for married as well as unwed mothers. From the perspective Geertz suggests to us, this is no small cargo of meaning. Furthermore, the French experience provides strong support for the proposition that, contrary to what one constantly hears from both sides of the abortion controversy in the United States, a divided society *can* compromise successfully on the abortion issue.[38]

In contrast to the current American legal situation, it is worth noting that the French statute *names* the underlying problem as one involving human life, not as a conflict involving a woman's individual liberty or privacy and a non-person. While showing great concern for the pregnant woman, it tries, through legal provisions of a type that have been struck down in a series of American cases, to make her aware of alternatives without either frightening or unduly burdening her. In 1983 the U.S. Supreme Court, in the *Akron* case, invalidated a city ordinance which contained a number of provisions similar to those in the 1975 French law, including an "informed consent" provision and a mandatory twenty-four-hour waiting period between the execution of the patient's consent form and the abortion procedure.[39] Justice Powell correctly observed that much of the information required by the city of Akron was "designed not to inform the woman's consent but rather to persuade her to withhold it altogether."[40] But the logic of the American abortion cases seemed to him to require that American states be forbidden to adopt, as France and other European countries have done, "abortion regulations designed to influence the woman's informed choice between abortion and childbirth."[41] A closely divided Supreme Court reaffirmed this position in 1986, holding unconstitutional the provisions of a Pennsylvania statute that would have required a pregnant woman, at least twenty-four hours before consenting to an abortion, to be informed about the availability of medical assistance and child support and of the fact that printed materials describing the fetus and listing agencies ready to help with alternatives to abortion were available for her inspection.[42] Even these mild provisions were considered by the majority in *Thornburgh v. American College of Obstetricians and Gynecologists* to be an impermissible "attempt to wedge the Commonwealth's message discouraging abortion into the privacy of the informed-consent dialogue between the woman and her physician."[43]

Since the Supreme Court seemed bent in these cases on preventing state legislatures from attempting in any way (except through denial of funding) to influence a woman's abortion decision, it is unlikely that a different approach to legislative drafting would have tipped the scale in either case. Still, it is worth noting that the informed consent provisions struck down in *Akron* and *Thornburgh* do communicate a somewhat different message from their French counterparts. While the information to be supplied in France stresses assistance to, and alternatives for, the pregnant woman, the Akron ordinance required that she be given information concerning the physical characteristics of the fetus, and both the Akron and the Pennsylvania legislation emphasized information about the risks to the woman of the surgical procedure. The tone of the French legislation is quite different. Akron's, and to a lesser extent, Pennsylvania's, abortion regulations seemed, in part at least, more threatening or anxiety-provoking, while France's are clearly meant to be helpful to the woman while trying to preserve the life of the fetus. If at some time in the future abortion regulation is returned to the American states, drafters of legislation in this area would do well to study foreign models, not only for their substance, but also for modes of expression. There are ways to combine compassion with affirmation of life.

The French manner of regulating abortion differs from the American in another way, which is typical of the West European approach to the problem. Most of the European statutes have tried to prevent abortion from becoming a routine procedure by discouraging the establishment of specialized abortion clinics. The United States Supreme Court, in contrast, has even struck down statutes which have attempted to require all second-trimester abortions to be performed in hospitals.[44] In its inability to see hospitalization requirements as anything other than a burden on the pregnant woman's freedom of choice, the Court in effect has abandoned the story it told in *Roe v. Wade* about the abortion decision as one to be reached in consultation between a woman and her personal physician.[45] At present, the majority of American abortions are performed in abortion facilities where the woman and doctor meet for the first time.[46] Only in America has a vast profit-making industry grown up around abortion.

France, as already mentioned, is but one of a large group of countries that permit abortion only for cause. Within this group, there are significant variations as to what grounds for abortion will be accepted. In Belgium, in theory at least, only an immediate and serious threat to the woman's life or health will support the defense of necessity. But in most other countries abortion is available, at least in the early stages of pregnancy, for what are often called the "hard" reasons—those having to do with the health of the mother, the condition of the fetus, and the circumstances under which pregnancy occurred. Commonly, the woman's mental health is specifically mentioned, or is read in by judicial interpretation.[47] Such countries permit abortion where it appears likely the woman will give birth to a child with a serious physical or mental defect,[48] or where the pregnancy is the result of a criminal offense against the woman.[49] Statutes in most of the countries which have taken the middle way also include "soft" reasons relating to economic or other circumstances that make continuation of the pregnancy a particular hardship for the woman involved or her family.[50] Most countries where abortion is permitted only for cause distinguish between early and late abortions, generally allowing abortions in the later stages of pregnancy only for the most serious reasons and establishing more procedural safeguards for the fetus.

An important variation among these countries concerns who has the last word on whether an adequate reason for abortion exists. For example, in France and Italy, in the early weeks the decision is entirely up to the woman. In England and Switzerland, two doctors must certify the existence of the grounds for abortion. In Greece, West Germany, Portugal, and Spain, even in early pregnancy, the existence of reasons must be confirmed by a doctor other than the one performing the abortion. In practice, it seems that so long as the woman can freely choose her doctor or doctors, medical discretion does not effectively restrict her choice. In the case of late abortions, however, many countries—even some of the "demand" jurisdictions—switch to another model in which an independent committee or board must certify the existence of serious reasons. In Canada, this is the system used for all abortions.

Some countries in the "for cause" group, such as France, Italy (whose 1978 abortion law is similar in tone and substance to the

French law described above),[51] and the Netherlands come close to sanctioning elective abortion. But the laws in all these countries differ ideologically from those in the so-called "abortion on demand" jurisdictions in that, even in the early stages of pregnancy, they insist that abortion is available only for serious reasons.

Abortion on Demand

Abortion in the early stages of pregnancy does not require any reason and is treated as the decision of the woman, or of the woman and her physician, in five West European countries (Austria, Denmark, Greece, Norway, and Sweden) and in the United States. The United States is alone in this group, however, in forbidding *any* state regulation of abortion for the sake of preserving the fetus until viability, which the Supreme Court in 1973 estimated at between twenty-four and twenty-eight weeks.[52] It is alone, too, in that even after viability, it does not *require* regulation to protect the fetus.[53] If a state does choose to try to preserve the life of the fetus after viability, it must observe the ruling in *Roe v. Wade* that state regulation may not interfere with abortions which are "necessary to preserve the life or health of the mother."[54] "Health," in Roe's companion case of *Doe v. Bolton,* is broadly understood as related to "all factors . . . relevant to the well-being of the patient."[55] Subsequent Supreme Court decisions have made clear that it will be very difficult for such legislation to pass constitutional muster. Pennsylvania's efforts to assure that viable fetuses be aborted alive if this can be done without significant medical risk to the mother, and to preserve the life and health of fetuses born alive during abortions, have twice come to grief.[56] In contrast, Austria, Denmark, Greece, and Norway all forbid abortion after the first trimester except for serious reasons,[57] while Sweden places the cut-off point for elective abortions somewhat later—at eighteen weeks.[58]

An examination of the least restrictive of these European elective abortion statutes indicates why it is inappropriate to characterize the United States as just one of several countries where abortion is available on demand. Even under the 1974 Swedish statute, which represents the extreme pro-choice end of the West European spectrum, we do not find the same studied rejection of efforts to preserve the fetus that characterizes the United States Supreme Court's abortion decisions. Abortion in Sweden is available upon the woman's request during the first eighteen weeks of pregnancy.[59] After the twelfth week, however, there is a mandatory consultation with a social worker.[60] Once eighteen weeks have passed, permission for abortion can be given only by the National Board of Health and Welfare and then only if there are "substantial grounds."[61] The Swedish statute specifically provides that abortions may not be performed at all if the fetus is likely to be viable, except when the woman's life or health is seriously endangered by the pregnancy.[62] In practice, it is said that the Board of Health and Welfare usually does not grant permission for abortions after the twenty-fourth week.[63] Furthermore, the 1974 abortion law forms part of a complex of legislation designed to promote birth control, with the express purpose of reducing abortion.[64] This group of laws liberalized abortion, but it also attempted to make sure the procedure would be a last resort by greatly expanding birth control education and information services and by reducing the cost of contraceptives. Some evidence of the effectiveness of this program is that, since the 1970s, both teenage abortions and the birth rate among teenagers have significantly decreased in Sweden.[65]

In comparing the United States to other countries where abortion is rather freely available, it is also important to keep in mind the messages that are being communicated by each country's child support and social welfare law. In Sweden, for example, although early abortion is unrestricted, generous social benefits put mothers, married or unmarried, in a financial position which is not merely at subsistence level, but quite strong. And Sweden's system for assessing and collecting child support from absent parents is perhaps the most effective in the world. Because Austria, Denmark, and Norway offer pregnant women significant support for choosing an alternative to abortion, they too can be said to offer more protection to unborn life than does the United States, even though their criminal law favors the mother's liberty over the fetus's life, at least in the early stages.

If we were to broaden our field of comparison to include the seven Warsaw Pact nations, we still would not find any country where there is so little restriction on abortion in principle as there is in the United States. The Soviet Union, Czechoslovakia, and East Germany all forbid abortion after the first trimester except for serious reasons,[66] while Bulgaria, Hungary, and Romania in recent years have made their abortion laws *more* restrictive.[67]

The foregoing survey makes clear that when the Supreme Court established a new American abortion policy in 1973, it did so in a way which put the United States in a class by itself, at least with respect to other developed nations. The decisions since 1973 have extended the right to abortion so far that former Chief Justice Burger concluded in 1986 that the concern expressed in *Roe v. Wade* for protection of potential life after viability was "mere shallow rhetoric."[68] Today, in order to find a country where the legal approach to abortion is as indifferent to unborn life as it is in the United States, we have to look to countries which are much less comparable to us politically, socially, culturally and economically, and where concern about population expansion overrides *both* women's liberty and fetal life. In China, for example, abortion is not punishable at all no matter when it takes place.[69] But this is part of a severe population control policy designed practically to compel couples to limit themselves to one child per family.[70]

Finally, it is worth noting here a point to which I will return later: it is rare, outside the United States, for elective abortion statutes to be characterized even by those who favor them as establishing a "right to abortion." The U.S. Supreme Court, however, after some initial equivocation in *Roe v. Wade,* now speaks quite routinely of a "constitutional right to abortion."[71] In the *Akron* case, the court reaffirmed what it called the "basic principle that a woman has a fundamental right to make the highly personal choice whether or not to terminate her pregnancy."[72]

ABORTION AS A CONSTITUTIONAL ISSUE

From the comparative point of view abortion policy in the United States appears singular, not only because it requires no protection of unborn life at any stage of pregnancy, in contrast to all the other countries with which we customarily compare ourselves, but also because our abortion policy was not worked out in the give-and-take of the legislative process. Our basic approach to, and our regulation of, abortion was established by the United States Supreme Court in a series of cases that rendered the abortion legislation of all states wholly or partly unconstitutional and severely limited the scope of future state regulation of abortion.[73] Although the abortion legislation of several other countries has been constitutionally challenged, only in Italy and in West Germany were the legislative resolutions of the problem held unconstitutional.[74] Nowhere have the courts gone so far as has the United States Supreme Court in precluding further statutory development.

The West German Constitutional Court Decision

The most famous of the European abortion decisions, that of the Constitutional Court of the Federal Republic of Germany,[75] is instructive both for its similarities to and differences from the American abortion cases. In 1974, as part of a general reform of its penal code, West Germany liberalized its abortion law to permit elective abortions in the first trimester.[76] Although abortion after the thirteenth day in principle remained a crime, a large exception decriminalized abortions before the end of the twelfth week, provided only that the pregnant woman first underwent counseling. As is typical of the few West European statutes that permit early abortion on demand, the 1974 West German law specified that abortions could be performed after the twelfth week only if there was certification of grave danger to the life or health of the pregnant woman or likelihood that serious and irreversible damage had already occurred to the fetus. In the United States, under *Roe v. Wade,* even such a broadly permissive regulation would be considered an unconstitutional invasion of the pregnant woman's right of privacy.[77] The law was challenged in West Germany, however, on the ground that complete decriminalization of abortion in the first trimester violated the right to life of the fetus. The challengers were the governments of five West German states and several legislators who had unsuccessfully opposed the statute in the Bundestag.[78] They relied primarily on Article 2(2) of the 1949 Constitution, known as the Basic Law, which states that

"Everyone shall have the right to life and to inviolability of his person," and on Article 1(1), which provides that it is the duty of the state to protect human dignity.[79]

The Second Senate of the West German Constitutional Court held, in a sixty-eight-page majority opinion, that "life developing within the womb" is constitutionally protected.[80] The court ruled (6 to 2) that the statute, to the extent that it permitted abortion without good reasons, violated Article 2(2), read in conjunction with Article 1(1), of the Basic Law.[81] In the hierarchy of constitutional values, the court held that human life is a central and supreme value of the constitutional order, to which the woman's acknowledged right to self-determination and privacy is subordinate.[82] The priority given to the value of life in the West German constitutional order is, the court explained, a reaction to the taking of innocent life in the years of the "final solution."[83] Not only the protection of life in Article 2(2), but also the express prohibition of the death penalty in Article 102, have to be read against the background of Germany's experience with a regime which classified certain forms of human life as worthless.[84] Both of these provisions, said the court, quoting one of its own earlier decisions, are "an affirmation of the fundamental value of human life and of a State concept that puts itself into emphatic opposition to the views of a political regime for which the individual life had little significance and which therefore practiced unlimited abuse in the name of the arrogated right over life and death of the citizen."[85]

What are the implications of holding that, at least from the fourteenth day after conception, the state is obliged to protect developing life? Since Article 2(2) of the Basic Law states that the right to life can only be abridged according to law, the court might have chosen to regard the 1974 statute as a legitimate abridgment, especially since the statute had attempted to strike a balance between the right to life and other constitutionally protected rights, such as liberty and the right to a sphere of privacy.[86] Nevertheless, the court held that the state not only must refrain from interfering with the developing life of the fetus, but must affirmatively act to protect it; furthermore, the legislature must use the criminal law to carry out this obligation where the protection mandated by the Constitution cannot be achieved in any other way.[87] There was thus no question of leaving first trimester abortions in a kind of law-free zone; abortion had to be expressly disapproved.[88] This did not mean, however, that all abortion had to be criminally punished. Indeed, the court hinted that perhaps the strict prior law, mitigated only by the defense of necessity, was unconstitutional, because its very severity led to lax enforcement, and thus did not sufficiently protect human life either.[89]

Basically, the court said, it is up to the legislature to decide what means to use to protect life.[90] Foremost among these means, however, should be welfare and social assistance:

> What can be done here and how the assistance measures are to be organized in detail are left in a large measure to the legislator and in general are removed from review by a constitutional court. In this context it will be principally a matter of strengthening the willingness of the person about to become a mother to accept the pregnancy with responsibility to self and to bring the fetus to full life. For all the State's duty to furnish protection, one may not lose sight of the fact that the developing life has, first of all, been entrusted by nature to the protection of the mother. It should be the most eminent purpose of government efforts on behalf of the protection of life to reawaken and, if necessary, strengthen the maternal protective will [in cases] where it has been lost. Admittedly, there are limits to the legislator's potential for influence in this area. Measures initiated by him often accomplish their purpose only indirectly and through lengthy educational work and the changes in societal attitudes and views which such educational work brings about.[91]

When and how the criminal law must be used in addition to social welfare measures is essentially a legislative decision, but since the legislature violated constitutional guarantees by completely decriminalizing first trimester abortions in the 1974 statute, the court gave it some guidance for the future. The criminal law must be used when the other means available to the legislature are inadequate for protecting developing life.[92] The court held that the counseling provisions of the 1974 act were not adequate for this purpose, but it is important to note that the court did leave open the possibility that some programs of counseling and material support might be devised so as to obviate the need to use the criminal law.[93]

When the criminal law is used to protect developing life, it is appropriate for the legislature to take other factors into consideration besides the value of fetal life. In some situations, especially where the pregnant woman's life or health is at stake, the court held it is permissible for the legislature to give priority to her interests.[94] Even where the woman's life or health is not seriously threatened, the relationship of a pregnant woman and a fetus is so interconnected and special that the legislature may properly consider what is "reasonably to be demanded" of the pregnant woman.[95] If the burden on the woman is truly extraordinary, the law need not require her to carry the pregnancy to term.[96] As examples of such extraordinary burdens, the court mentioned cases where the fetus is likely to be born with a grave defect, where the pregnancy resulted from a criminal act against the woman, or where the pregnancy has grave implications for the "general social situation of the pregnant woman and her family."[97] "The decisive point is that in all these cases another interest equally worthy of protection by the Constitution asserts itself with such urgency that the State's legal order cannot demand here that the pregnant woman under all circumstances concede preeminence to the right of the unborn."[98] Thus the legislature was left free to remove quite a broad range of cases from punishment without violating constitutional norms. It must do so, however, in a way that proceeds in principle "from a duty of bringing the pregnancy to term" and treating "its termination as a wrong."[99] "The false impression must be avoided that termination of pregnancy involves the same social [significance] as say a trip to the physician for the purpose of healing an illness, or even that it involves a legally irrelevant alternative to contraception."[100]

What is important is that the *totality* of abortion regulations— that is, all criminal, public health, and social welfare laws relating to abortion—be in proportion to the importance of the legal value of life, and that, as a whole, they work for the continuation of the pregnancy.[101] The 1974 statute violated the Constitution because, although it substituted preventive counseling for all penal sanctions in the first twelve weeks, it did not sufficiently register disapproval of abortion in principle.[102]

Pending the enactment of appropriate legislation, the court announced its own set of "transitional rules," which gave a fairly good indication of what it thought was "reasonably to be demanded" of the pregnant woman. Under these rules, abortions performed during the first twelve weeks were permitted under the same conditions that the 1974 legislation had established for later abortions, with two additions.[103] Abortions in the first twelve weeks were to be exempted from criminal punishment not only in cases of probable danger to the mother's life or grave injury to her health, or likelihood that the child would be born with a serious defect, but also where the pregnancy resulted from a criminal offense against the woman, or where the abortion was sought "in order to avert the danger of a grave emergency to the pregnant woman which could not be averted in another manner which she may [reasonably] be required to risk."[104]

When one compares these rules with the 1974 statute that was held invalid, the likely difference in practice does not appear to be very great. Yet the distinction between complete decriminalization and exemption from punishment where serious reasons are present was crucial to the court in a way that a student of culture like Geertz would readily appreciate. Throughout its lengthy opinion, the West German court appears to have accepted a view of criminal law as a way of affirming the moral order of society and as an embodiment of ideals of right conduct. Explaining why abortion cannot be completely decriminalized or made the subject of a merely formal condemnation in the early months, the court said:

> If one views as the task of the penal law the protection of especially important legal values and elementary values of the community, a great importance accrues to its function. Just as important as the observable reaction in an individual case is the long range effect of a penal norm, which in its principal normative content ("abortion is punishable") has existed for a very long time. No doubt, the mere existence of such a penal sanction has influence on the conceptions of value and the manner of behavior of the populace . . . If the threat of punishment disappears in its entirety, the impression will arise of necessity in the consciousness of the citizens of the state that in all cases the interruption of pregnancy is legally allowed and, therefore, even from a socio-ethical point of view, is no longer to be condemned . . .[105]

The West German Court was manifestly concerned about the possible effect of a change in the law on ideas and behavior, unlike Justice Blackmun who in *Roe* brushed off values and moral attitudes as among the many factors which "tend to complicate and not to simplify the problem."[106]

As for the fact that the 1974 law was said to be consistent with abortion regulation in several other "democratic countries in the Western world,"[107] including the United States, the Constitutional Court observed that such considerations could not influence its decision because:

> Underlying the Basic Law are principles for the structuring of the state that may be understood only in the light of the historical experience and the spiritual-moral confrontation with the previous system of National Socialism ... At its basis lies the concept ... that human beings possess an inherent worth as individuals in the order of creation which uncompromisingly demands unconditional respect for the life of every individual human being, even for the apparently socially "worthless," and which therefore excludes destruction of such life without legally justifiable grounds. This fundamental constitutional decision determines the structure and interpretation of the entire legal order ... Even a general change of the viewpoints dominant in the populace on this subject—if such a change could be established at all—would change nothing.[108]

It is noteworthy that even the dissenters, after remarking that the United States Supreme Court had held that criminal punishment of abortion in the first trimester was a violation of a fundamental right of the woman, stated: "This would, under German constitutional law, go too far indeed."[109]

The two dissenting judges (one of them the only woman on the Constitutional Court) criticized the West German decision in terms that sound very familiar to American lawyers. Echoing the dissenters and the academic critics of *Roe v. Wade,* they said that the majority, at the instance of a defeated legislative minority, had simply substituted its own conception of value for that of the democratically elected branch.[110] It was especially regrettable, they added, that on such a controversial question as abortion the decision should not have been left to the compromise and trial-and-error of the legislative process.[111] While agreeing that the fetus, at least after fourteen days, was "developing human life" and that the state was required by the constitution to protect it, they argued that the court is neither competent nor equipped to tell the legislature *how* it must do so.[112]

In addition to provoking a rare published dissent within the court, the West German decision did not at first seem to be welcomed outside it either. Soon after the decision, the Constitutional Court building in Karlsruhe was bombed, with a revolutionary women's group claiming credit.[113] Pro-life forces, on the other hand, could hardly have been pleased with the court's willingness to balance the life of the fetus against mere hardship to the pregnant woman. For its part, the federal government, which had sponsored the 1974 legislation, issued an official statement on the day the decision was announced insisting that its arguments in favor of the constitutionality of the law had been "inalterably sound and conclusive," and stressing that the law had been in harmony with similar reforms in other countries.[114] According to public opinion polls at the time, half the population regretted the court's opinion, 32 percent welcomed it, and 18 percent had no opinion.[115] These immediate reactions were followed, however, as in France, by compromise legislation and a period of eleven years in which debate has continued, but without the sporadic violence that has marred the American scene.

In 1976 the West German parliament amended the criminal code to conform to the guidelines laid down in the 1975 decision.[116] As a result, West German abortion law is presently typical of that in force in the broad middle range of the twenty countries whose law has been examined for this chapter. Abortion is permitted in the first trimester if the pregnancy resulted from an illegal act against the woman or if it places the woman in a situation of serious hardship that cannot be averted any other way; abortion is permitted up to the twenty-second week if there are serious reasons for presuming the child will be born with such a severe defect that the woman cannot reasonably be required to continue with the pregnancy; and abortion is permitted at any time if there is a serious danger to the life or physical or mental health of the woman which cannot be averted any other way she can reasonably be required to bear.[117] As in France, any woman seeking an abortion must first undergo counseling during which she is to be advised of services that would facilitate the continuation of the pregnancy.[118] A three-day waiting period after such counseling is also required.[119] As is typical in West European abortion legislation generally, the statute provides stricter penalties for the person who performs an illegal abortion than for the woman who consents to it.[120]

The West German Constitutional Court decision and the 1976 West German abortion statute were both challenged in 1977 before the European Commission of Human Rights on the ground that they interfered with the right to respect for private life guaranteed under Article 8 of the European Convention on Human Rights.[121] This article provides that public authorities may not interfere with the right of private life except where necessary for, among other things, "protection of health or morals, or for the protection of the rights and freedoms of others."[122] The commission, pointing out that the right to privacy in Article 8 is not absolute, held, with one dissent, that since the pregnant woman's private life is "closely connected with the developing fetus," the legal rules in question did not violate Article 8.[123] In support of its conclusion that Article 8 could not be interpreted to mean that abortion is a matter solely pertaining to the private life of the woman, the commission pointed out that every member state of the European Convention regulated abortion at the time the convention went into effect. It found "no evidence that it was the intention of the parties to the Convention to bind themselves in favor of any particular solution" among the many that were being discussed and proposed at that time.[124]

As in the United States, the constitutional decision in West Germany on the grounds for abortion has been followed by controversies about funding. The question in the Federal Republic, however, is whether the present Social Security law which stipulates that national medical insurance covers lawfully (*rechtsmässig*) performed abortions is constitutional as applied to abortions that are not viewed as medically necessary.[125] This issue turns in part on whether those abortions which have been decriminalized under the criminal code can be said to be lawful, as opposed to merely being excused from punishment. Academic opinion is divided on whether the withdrawal of criminal punishment for some abortions means that they are therefore legal. However, the constitutional requirement of protection of unborn life, together with the fact that the criminal code makes all abortion illegal in principle seems to militate against the idea that abortions within the exceptions are justifiable as distinct from merely excused.[126] It is one thing to recognize, as did Aristotle, that when we do what we ought not to do under pressure that overstrains ordinary human nature, pardon is appropriate.[127] It is another matter to say that extenuating circumstances can make an otherwise wrongful act rightful. Those in West Germany who oppose public funding for medically unnecessary abortions are concerned that such financing reinforces in society the very notion the Constitutional Court was intent on refuting: that abortion is just an ordinary medical procedure.[128]

Messages of the Constitutional Decisions

Both the West German Constitutional Court in 1975 and the United States Supreme Court in 1973 set aside the decisions of elected legislatures on the abortion question. Both landmark decisions ultimately rested less on constitutional language, intent of the framers, or prior judicial interpretation of the constitutions involved than they did on the authority of the courts themselves. Both courts engaged in a type of general rule-making activity more commonly associated with the legislature than the judiciary: the U.S. Supreme Court by dividing pregnancy into trimesters with specific rules assigned to each, and the West German court by promulgating its own transitional regulations.[129] Both majority opinions were subjected to the same sorts of process-based criticism from dissenters and the academic legal community for allegedly having substituted the judges' own notions of value and utility for those of the more representative branch of government.

The differences between the two decisions, however, are more interesting than the similarities. The differences go well beyond the obvious one in outcome: the court in the United States held that restrictive state legislation impinged on a fundamental right of the pregnant woman, while the West German court found that a liberal federal statute did not sufficiently protect unborn life. In the first place, the West German court left the legislature with considerable room to devise, and in the future, if it wishes, to revise, abortion policy, providing only that abortion is not to be completely decriminalized unless adequate alternative preventive measures are in place, and that the total effect of the laws in the area is to support and protect the value of human life. Within this framework, the Bundestag was able to work out a compromise typical of that reached at this stage in history by most other Western nations. *Roe v. Wade* and succeeding cases, on the other hand, have virtually closed down the state legislative process with respect to abortions prior to viability. Legislative attempts to provide for more information, deliberation, and counseling, more participation by others in the woman's decision-making process, and even protection for the fetus after viability have regularly been struck down.

A second difference is that each court imagined the facts of abortion quite differently. The West German court characterized the situation as one in which, at least after the fourteenth day, developing human life is at stake. This immediately thrust the court into the kind of issue the United States Supreme Court did not wish to face. In West Germany the question is: Under what circumstances is it permissible to take human life? Within our own constitutional framework, it would have been: What are the due process rights of a fetus? But that question was avoided. Rather than concentrate on the potential application of the Fourteenth Amendment language providing that states shall not "deprive any person of life . . . without due process of law," the United States Supreme Court chose to characterize the facts so that they did not come within the scope of the amendment. Justice Blackmun carefully avoided describing the fetus as either human or alive.[130] By doing so, however, he delivered a potent message. Legal specialists may understand that to say a fetus is not a "person" within the meaning of the Fourteenth Amendment says nothing at all about the essential nature of the fetus for other purposes. (Blacks have been held by American courts not to be "people" or "citizens," and women have been held not to be "persons.")[131] But as *Roe v. Wade* is filtered through the communications media to popular consciousness, the statement by the highest court of the land that a fetus is not a "person" has great potential for being misunderstood.

The third difference is that although both courts substituted a set of values for those promoted by the respective legislatures, the content of those values differs markedly. *Roe v. Wade,* like its predecessor, *Eisenstadt v. Baird,*[132] embodies a view of society as a collection of separate autonomous individuals.[133] The West German decision emphasizes the connections among the woman, developing life, and the larger community. Donald Kommers has therefore characterized the difference between the two decisions as one between individualistic and communitarian values.[134] He points to *Roe*'s emphasis on the individual woman, her privacy and autonomy (not to mention Justice Douglas's equating privacy with "preferred life style"),[135] and contrasts it with the West German court's emphasis on the interest that society as a whole has, not only in the abortion decision itself, but in the long-range formation of beliefs and attitudes about human life.

Kommers' point is quite different from the familiar process-based critique of *Roe* in the academic legal community. His criticism is not based on the idea that the court should have deferred to the legislature. Kommers, in fact, might well agree with Laurence Tribe, a *Roe* defender, that the Supreme Court's voice should be heard on the difficult unresolved questions that divide our society, and that the court should participate in the "evolution of moral and thus legal consciousness."[136] Kommers seems concerned, however, about the long-range effects of the substantive position taken by the Supreme Court. From the point of view of those who do not object to the court assuming the role of moral arbiter, the West German court thus should get credit for doing precisely what Archibald Cox criticized the United States Supreme Court for failing to do in *Roe*. It articulated "principles sufficiently absolute to give them roots throughout the community and continuity over significant periods of time, and to lift them above the level of the pragmatic political judgments of a particular time and place."[137]

One cannot distinguish what the two courts did, in this respect, by saying that the West German court imposes a certain version of morality upon pregnant women, while the American court leaves the moral decision up to the individual woman herself. The notion that abortion is an individual and private decision is itself a moral notion. The problem is, which version of morality should prevail? The moral basis for preferring the values of toleration and freedom of choice when other important values are also at stake is beginning to seem increasingly unclear.[138]

A fourth difference between the decisions concerns the role played by and the meaning given to the idea of privacy. Unlike the American Constitution, the West German Basic Law of 1949 expressly protects something very like what we call the right to privacy. In the United States the right of an individual to protection of a certain intimate sphere from outside interference has entered constitutional law rather recently by judicial interpretation, though privacy as a legal idea had been around for some time. In 1890, probably under the influence of John Stuart Mill's well-known defense of the right of an individual to be free from intrusion into his personal life, Warren and Brandeis published their famous law review article titled, "The Right to Privacy."[139] In it they reviewed a number of English and American cases involving intellectual and artistic property and claimed that, properly understood, they all involved a fundamental right which the authors characterized as "the right to be let alone."[140] This concept soon found acceptance in American tort law, and eventually migrated into Supreme Court opinions. In 1965 some of the Justices in *Griswold v. Connecticut* perceived a right to privacy lurking in the "penumbra" of certain clauses of the Constitution.[141]

Following *Griswold,* the scope and precise content of the new constitutional right was unclear. Since the case had struck down Connecticut birth control laws as applied to married persons, it seemed at first that the right of privacy might be some kind of family right, protecting married couples from governmental intrusion into the sphere of procreation. That the right was not so limited was made plain in the 1972 case of *Eisenstadt v. Baird,* where the court specified that the new right was an individual right: "If the right of privacy means anything, it is the right of an *individual,* married or single, to be free from unwarranted governmental intrusion into matters so fundamentally affecting a person as the decision whether to bear or beget a child."[142] Then, one year after *Eisenstadt,* the right of privacy was dramatically extended in *Roe v. Wade* to cover a pregnant woman's decision whether or not to have an abortion.[143]

As in the United States, the right of privacy entered the legal system in Germany through tort law. The creation of a cause of action for invasion of privacy was one of the great innovations of German case law.[144] But when privacy was taken into West German constitutional law in 1949, it was given a somewhat different meaning from the one its American counterpart came to have. Privacy rights in West German constitutional law are based on Article 2(1) of the Basic Law ("Everyone shall have the right to the free development of his personality, insofar as he does not violate the rights of others or offend against the constitutional order or the moral code") in conjunction with Article 1(1) ("The dignity of man shall be inviolable"). The affirmative German right to the free development of one's personality contrasts with the negative American formulation of privacy as a right to be left alone. Whereas the American conceptualization of privacy emphasizes freedom *from* various kinds of restraints, the German version stresses and makes clear what this freedom is *for.* As it turns out, the freedom is for an individualistic value: the development of the human person. But at the same time, the German idea of privacy suggests a social dimension (since a "personality" cannot develop fully in the absence of relationships with other human beings), whereas the American right emphasizes the isolated individual.

Specifying what individual freedom is for makes it possible to begin to work out distinctions between liberty and license, by referring to the purpose for which freedom is claimed.[145] The West German privacy right is expressly limited in its very inception by the "rights of others," "the constitutional order," and the "moral code." The Federal Constitutional Court has emphasized the qualified nature of the right:

> If an individual in his capacity as a citizen living within a community enters into relations with others, influences others by his existence or activity and thereby impinges upon the personal sphere of other people or upon the interests of communal life, his exclusive right to be the master of his own private sphere may become subject

to restrictions unless his sacrosanct innermost sphere of life is concerned.[146]

By contrast, the Supreme Court of the United States, in elaborating the right of privacy, has neither explained the theory upon which the right is based nor shown how it might be limited until 1986, when the court declined to hold that homosexual sodomy was within its scope.[147] Thus the right of privacy, which is so bound up with individual autonomy and isolation, has become one of the most absolute rights known to the American legal system.

Finally, a striking difference between the West German and American abortion decisions is the relative lack of emphasis on rights in the former and the key role that rights play in the latter. Although the West German Basic Law explicitly protects the "right to life," the Constitutional Court chose to emphasize the character of this right as a value of the community rather than as something that belongs to the fetus. The court was more concerned with the obligation of the state to promote the public value than it was with any rights the value might give to individuals. A similar approach was taken in the April 1985 decision of the Spanish Constitutional Court substantially upholding a statute that repealed one of the last of the very restrictive European abortion laws.[148] The Spanish court's opinion shows the unmistakable influence of the 1975 West German decision. The Spanish Constitution, like the West German Basic Law, contains a right to life, which the court characterized as "the" fundamental constitutional value. However, the court expressly declined to hold that a fetus has legal rights. Rather, the court said that unborn life is a public good protected by the Constitution. This gives rise to an obligation on the part of the state to make that protection effective through law, including, where necessary, the criminal law. The Spanish statute in question amended the Penal Code so as to exempt from punishment abortions carried out for the usual three "hard" reasons: life or health of the mother, rape or incest, and likelihood that the child would be born with serious defects. Like the West German court, the Spanish court held that the legislature need not impose penal sanctions for abortion when continuation of the pregnancy would constitute an insupportable hardship for the woman concerned. The court had no difficulty finding that the three statutory exceptions from punishment were constitutionally permissible.

As Richard Stith has pointed out, the West German and Spanish constitutional courts, instead of balancing individual rights, emphasize a commitment to an order of values. In both opinions, but even more emphatically in the Spanish, there is the notion that what the pregnant woman can be required to sacrifice for the common value is related to what the social welfare state is ready and able to do to help with the burdens of childbirth and parenthood. For example, the Spanish court, reluctantly upholding the exception for a defective fetus, takes note of the hardship involved in raising a disabled child and the very limited degree of public assistance presently available in Spain. The statement intimates that the exception would need to be re-examined if and when the social state were able to alleviate the strain of raising disabled children.

Against this background, it becomes possible to identify yet another common fallacy in discussions of the American abortion debate: that, in Kristin Luker's words, "the two sides share almost no common premises and very little common language."[149] In fact, pro-life and pro-choice activists, along with the United States Supreme Court, share several familiar premises and terms about individuals and rights that are in marked contrast to the way the West German and Spanish courts have approached the subject of abortion. Quite consistently with what Robert Bellah and his co-investigators report in their recent book, *Habits of the Heart,*[150] most Americans think of abortion issues as involving individual rights—either the right to life of the fetus or a woman's right to privacy, choice, or control over her own body. Thus the two seemingly irrevocably opposed positions are actually locked within the same intellectual framework, a framework that appears rather rigid and impoverished when viewed from a comparative perspective.

WHAT WE MIGHT LEARN FROM
EUROPEAN EXPERIENCES

The foregoing survey demonstrates that two very widely held beliefs on the abortion question are erroneous. The first is that the present legal situation in the United States with respect to abortion is not particularly unusual. The second is that on this issue no compromise is possible. One hears this latter misconception not only from those who identify themselves as pro-life or pro-choice, but also from many who have tried to analyze the problem from an Olympian point of view. Gilbert Steiner wrote in 1981, "Abortion can be counted on to be the dominant family-related public problem for the indefinite future, and the one the policy process is least likely to resolve, because neither side is comfortable with less than total victory, each side views its cause as sacred, and both are right."[151] For people who believe they have achieved certainty about the moral issues involved, it may well be true that compromise of their moral position is unthinkable. But the experience of other societies that have been just as deeply divided as ours, if not more so, on the abortion question, shows that when the legislative process is allowed to operate, *political* compromise is not only possible but typical. These compromises, reached in the usual democratic way, are not entirely satisfactory to everyone. They distinguish between early and late abortions by drawing a line that is difficult to defend on rational grounds, and they weigh the competing interests in a way that is apt to be distasteful to pro-life and pro-choice activists alike. But the European countries have been able to live relatively peacefully with these laws without experiencing the violence born of complete frustration and without foreclosing re-examination and renegotiation of the issues.

The Continuing Consensus

Brigitte and Peter Berger write in their recent book on family policy: "Any new consensus on [the abortion] issue will emerge from common reflection about uncertainties, rather than from shared certitude."[152] Taking this as a starting point, it seems likely, according to the public opinion surveys, that a consensus based on uncertainty has been present all along in the United

States. It is not particularly difficult to ascertain where the public stands on abortion since the three principal surveys, National Fertility Studies, Gallup, and National Opinion Research Center, have exhibited major similarities over many years.[153] Both before and after *Roe,* majorities (consistently around 55 percent) have been opposed to its major innovation, elective abortion, and to much of the content of *Roe* and other abortion decisions.[154] At the same time, majorities have consistently opposed a total ban on abortion and believe that the law should specify the circumstances under which it is permissible.[155] They strongly approve abortion if the woman's health is in danger, and disapprove if it is sought for no other reason than that the woman does not want the child.[156] Majorities, women more than men, disapprove of abortion after the first trimester.[157] Majorities believe that human life begins before birth, with men more likely to see life beginning later than women do.[158]

As Blake has pointed out, the public view of abortion is "both at odds with that of the Supreme Court and at variance with what the Court believed public opinion to be."[159] A 1983 summary of the survey data shows that the intense public controversy over abortion has produced little overall change in attitudes about legalizing abortion since 1974.[160] There is little support for making all abortions illegal and little support for unrestricted freedom of choice. Support for legalized abortion depends on the reasons for abortion and when in the pregnancy it is performed.[161]

Public opinion thus does not support the positions of most activists in the pro-life or pro-choice movements. The surveys indicate that most of us feel uncertainty and ambivalence concerning the abortion issue. Sidney and Daniel Callahan have usefully pointed out that sympathizers with one or the other side of the abortion controversy are not so easily classified as are militants: "The more complex reality is that many in the pro-life group will not condemn out of hand all women who have abortions; and many in the pro-choice group are repelled by the banal moral arguments used to justify many abortions."[162] But uncertainty about one's position, as the opinion surveys make plain, is not the same as indifference or moral relativism. Unlike most partisans on either side, the public seems to believe that there is an important difference between early and late stages of gestation and that the value of unborn life should be weighed along with competing claims and values. As Daniel Degnan pointed out in 1974, these two notions would have to form the basis of any political compromise on the abortion question.[163]

For the United States to return to the point where compromise legislation could be threshed out in the state legislatures, we would need either a constitutional amendment to that effect,[164] or, preferably, the Supreme Court's reconsideration of its own rulings. Both these alternatives are often said to be unlikely. But vigorous political pursuit of an amendment, along with several other factors, including medical advances, has made the prospect of the Supreme Court's eventual re-examination of *Roe* and its progeny increasingly thinkable. It is true that *Roe v. Wade* was expressly reaffirmed in 1983, and again in 1986.[165] But since *Roe* was decided (7 to 2) in 1973, Justice O'Connor joined the court and became an important third dissenter (along with Justice White and now Chief Justice Rehnquist) from the doctrine of the abortion cases. Justice Scalia is likely to be a fourth. Moreover, the gradual change of views of the former Chief Justice, who concurred in *Roe* and *Doe,* may be indicative of the ripeness of this line of cases for complete rethinking. Former Chief Justice Burger, who would not go along with the majority in *Danforth* and *Colautti v. Franklin,* came close in his dissenting opinion in *Thornburgh* to repudiating not only the progeny, but *Roe* itself.[166]

It would not be necessary to overrule *Roe* in order to achieve the result of returning most regulation of abortion to the states. The narrow holding of *Roe* was simply that the Texas abortion statute was unconstitutional. The Texas statute, typical of older state laws on abortion, made all abortions illegal except to save the life of the mother.[167] If a similar statute had come before the West German Constitutional Court, it is entirely possible it would have been held unconstitutional there too. By prohibiting all early abortions except in the gravest of circumstances, statutes of this type may, at one and the same time, unduly burden the pregnant woman *and* fail to promote the state's interest in potential life. In striking down the Texas statute, the Supreme Court need not have banned *all* regulation in the interest of the fetus in the first two trimesters.

It could have authorized the states, within broad limits, to work out legislation which would have treated the abortion question in all its complexity and with the gravity it deserves.

Without overruling, then, the court could, in time-honored fashion, confine *Roe* to its narrow holding. Here the Italian experience is instructive. In 1975 the Italian Constitutional Court was asked to rule on the constitutionality of an article of the Penal Code which made all abortions criminal except where the defense of strict necessity applied. The court held that the Penal Code could not constitutionally place "a total and absolute priority" on the fetus's constitutional right to life where this would deny adequate protection to the pregnant woman's health, which is also an interest protected under the Italian Constitution.[168] This narrow holding permitted the Italian legislature to adopt compromise legislation (similar to the French statutes discussed above), which has been well accepted in a country where abortion was an explosive political issue.[169]

The three dissenters in *Akron* already have taken a narrow view of *Roe*. In an opinion written by Justice O'Connor, and joined by Justices White and Rehnquist, they argued that the state's compelling interest in potential life is "present *throughout* pregnancy" and not merely in the last trimester.[170] But, Justice O'Connor said, "not every regulation that the State imposes must be measured against the State's compelling interests and examined with strict scrutiny."[171] The appropriate forum for resolution of such an extremely sensitive issue as abortion, she maintained, is not the court but the state legislature.[172] She also pointed out an inherent weakness of the *Roe* decision. If, as *Roe* says, state regulation in the interest of the fetus becomes "compelling" at "viability," fast-moving developments in medical technology can be expected to move the point at which such regulation is proper further and further back.[173] But since medical advances have made second trimester abortions increasingly safer for the mother, regulation in her interest is less needed than it was in 1973. Thus, Justice O'Connor has stated, *Roe v. Wade* "is clearly on a collision course with itself."[174]

Perhaps—when and if *Roe* self-destructs—out of its wreckage can be devised a set of guiding principles for state legislatures, in which the state's interest in "potential life" is given due weight throughout pregnancy and the woman's liberty or privacy interests are also taken into account, without, however, being elevated to their present near-absolute status. Of course, the problem is complicated in the United States by the fact that *Roe*-like holdings could be expected from some state supreme courts under state constitutions. Obviously, all that is said here with respect to the desirability of leaving the matter open for legislative decision-making applies to state as well as federal courts.

As time passes, not only does the *Roe* decision appear to be collapsing from within, but the opinions of leading constitutional law writers, many of them not opposed to abortion in principle, have been marshaled against it. Archibald Cox, Alexander Bickel, John Hart Ely, Harry Wellington, Richard Epstein, and Paul Freund have all been highly critical.[175] Furthermore, at least two of *Roe*'s prominent defenders, would, I believe, also be opposed to it if they consistently applied their own theories of constitutional hermeneutics to that case. Laurence Tribe and Michael Perry were both so intent on refuting criticisms of *Roe* based on what they consider to be false notions about the proper roles of courts and legislatures that they lost sight of the ways in which *Roe* offends their own ideas of what the Supreme Court ought to be doing. (Tribe, indeed, later recanted his major reason for approving of the decision and remains only a lukewarm supporter.)[176] Both Tribe and Perry assert that the Supreme Court should participate as one important set of voices in the continuing social dialogue on vital public issues.[177] It would appear, therefore, that they, to a greater degree than other more "interpretivist" scholars, should be opposed to the court's participating in such a way as to close off discussion once it has spoken.[178]

In one of his earlier articles, Perry had argued that it was legitimate and desirable for the Supreme Court to decide cases on the basis of ethical principles that it discovers in conventional morality.[179] Of *Roe v. Wade* he wrote, "It seems quite clear that the Court's implicit evaluation of conventional moral culture vis-à-vis restrictive abortion legislation was essentially accurate."[180] In support of this confident judgment, he cited only an NBC News report of a 1974 election day exit poll.[181] Leaving aside the difficult question of the relation of public opinion to conventional morality, or to adjudication, we have already seen that public opinion only supports the narrow holding of *Roe*. There is no evidence at all that "conventional moral culture" validates the fundamental and radical message of *Roe* and *Doe* that *no* state regulation of abortion in the interest of preserving unborn life is permissible in approximately the first six months of pregnancy, and that such regulation in the last trimester is permissible only if it does not interfere with the woman's physical and mental well-being.

In two later articles Perry has quoted with approval Alfred North Whitehead's statement: "The art of free society . . . consists first in the maintenance of the symbolic code, and secondly, in fearlessness of revision . . . Those societies which cannot combine reverence to their symbols with freedom of revision must ultimately decay."[182] Because Perry himself views the Constitution as our "symbolic code" and the Supreme Court as "an active participant" in its fearless revision,[183] he should be sympathetic to the views expressed here. His notion that the court should play an important role "in the effort to reachieve the 'Constitution' in every generation"[184] seems closely related to the hermeneutical vision of White and Geertz.

By calling our attention to the way in which law endows social action with meaning, Geertz's and White's insights reinforce the position that in the absence of a clear constitutional mandate controversial matters like regulation of abortion should not be prematurely constitutionalized. Litigation, like the legislative processes of bargaining, education, and persuasion, can contribute to the way in which a society collectively imagines reality—and revises that imagination as knowledge and experience increase. But if the courts unnecessarily decide such controversies on constitutional grounds, these potentially creative and collaborative processes are brought to a halt. The main avenue left open for *political* activity with respect to the abortion issue is then the cumbersome process of constitutional amendment.

Compromise legislation would of course be displeasing to many. A by-product of certitude is often an insistence upon total victory. For some among the pro-choice advocates, any retrenchment from the unconditional victory they won in 1973 would be felt as a stinging defeat. To perhaps many more among the pro-life forces, such laws would be seen as unacceptably relativizing human life. Physicians could be expected to resent any withdrawal of their absolute discretion as much as their re-exposure to possible criminal liability. But the opinion polls strongly indicate that such legislation would be supported by the majority of American women and men. Few people who favor the woman's right to choose contend that the fetus in late pregnancy deserves no legal protection at all. Most pro-life advocates, on the other hand, accept abortion even in late pregnancy to preserve the life of the pregnant woman. Many in the pro-life ranks, moreover, are beginning to realize that in our pluralistic society it may not be possible fully to protect fetal life. As they consider what laws have a realistic chance of being adopted and accepted, some are coming to the view that, between the doctrine of the abortion cases, under which unborn life is of little or no value, and a law which permits abortions only for serious reasons, compromise legislation is the lesser of evils. A wise and moderate pro-life supporter, Daniel Degnan, has written that compromise laws "not only can be supported [by those who believe all abortion is morally wrong], but there may even be a duty to support them in the present circumstances."[185] One need not agree with Aristotle that the lesser evil, in comparison with the greater evil, is to be reckoned as a good,[186] in order to prefer it. Perhaps it is fitting that abortion law at present should mirror our wonder as well as our ignorance about the mystery of life, our compassion for women who may be frightened and lonely in the face of a major crisis, and our instinctive uneasiness at terminating a form of innocent human life, whether we call it a fetus, an embryo, a baby, or an unborn child.

In Western Europe, as in the American states before *Roe v. Wade,* compromise has not eliminated controversy about abortion law. Intense discussion continues, but without what Guido Calabresi has called the "sense of desperate embattlement" that has characterized the debate in the United States after *Roe.*[187] Calabresi has, I believe, identified some important reasons for this difference. The abortion debate on both sides involves cherished beliefs of groups that view themselves as mistreated in American society—particularly women and some ethnic communities.[188]

Kristin Luker has added the insight that for the women who now constitute the great majority of activists in both camps, values central to their lives are at stake.[189] In this situation, Calabresi argues sensibly, it is desirable not to reject the ideals of the losers as invalid or outside the law.

> A decision which recognizes the values on the losing side as real and significant tends to keep us from becoming callous with respect to the moralisms and beliefs that lose out . . . [I]t can even lead to a strengthening of those values. It can exert a favorable gravitational pull and create a climate of opinion which will lead courts and legislatures to uphold the losing values in contexts in which the winning values are not at stake. This gives the losers hope that the values they cherish will not be ultimately abandoned by the society, and that the society, despite what it chooses to do now, will not become immoral in the long run. It tells the losers that, though they lost, they and their values do carry weight and are recognized in our society, even when they don't win out. In other words, it treats [them] as citizens of the polity and not as emarginated bigots or unassimilated immigrants.[190]

These words of wisdom appear to be addressed to majorities, exhorting them not to ride roughshod over minority views even when they have prevailed in the democratic process. The problem of abortion regulation in the United States is immeasurably aggravated, however, by the fact that the extreme position of the Supreme Court in the abortion cases represents the views of only a minority of Americans.

A decision leaving abortion regulation basically up to state legislatures would have encouraged constructive activity by partisans of both sides. The European experience bears out this conjecture. Since the basic statutory changes of the 1970s were put in place, many countries have made major and minor legal adjustments without undue acrimony. Nor are all these changes moving inexorably in one direction. Norway, which adopted a liberal "for cause" statute in 1975, shifted to elective early abortion in 1978. Finland and Japan in recent years both have reduced the length of the period in early pregnancy during which abortion is rather freely available.

We can get some idea of what compromise legislation in the

United States might look like by speculating about how matters would stand today if the Supreme Court in 1973 (and other courts) had left the states basically free within broad limits to work out their own abortion policies. Several clues appear as we consider what the states were already in the process of doing when *Roe* and *Doe* were decided and what other Western countries have done since the early 1970s. By the time of *Roe v. Wade* in 1973, abortion law in the United States, as in the rest of the developed world, was in ferment.[191] True, most states had not yet revised their criminal laws, which typically permitted abortion only to save the life of the mother.[192] There is every reason to think, however, that statutes of the Texas or even the Georgia type struck down in *Roe* and *Doe* would not have survived long. Starting in 1967, nineteen states had changed their laws by 1973, as had England, Canada, and most Australian states.[193]

The situation was analogous to that of divorce law in the preceding decade. Strict divorce laws were on the books of most states in the 1960s, but had been eroded in practice by collusion, establishing "residence" in other states with more liberal grounds for divorce, and most of all by relaxed judicial interpretation and application of the grounds for divorce.[194] By 1985 no states had exclusively fault-based divorce anymore, but only a minority had moved to exclusively nonfault divorce.[195] The majority had settled for a compromise, combining nonfault with traditional grounds.[196] Most states still preserve the notion, however attenuated, that society has an interest in the institution of marriage and in the means of its termination. With regard to abortion, it was fairly predictable that the activity of the American Law Institute,[197] the Uniform Law Commissioners,[198] the state legislatures, interest groups, and interested individuals of all sorts would have produced a similar pattern. As with divorce law in the 1960s, restrictive abortion laws in the early 1970s were being undermined by collusion between doctor and patient, by travel for those who had the means to do so, and by liberal interpretations of what constituted a threat to the life or health of the pregnant woman. This interpretive shift, it might be argued, marked the decisive transition to making abortions widely available, just as judicial transformation of the cruelty ground for divorce to include mental cruelty was what made divorce readily available. To a great extent, later statutory changes in both areas simply consolidated previous practices.

Regarding abortion, this process of change was well under way in the United States in 1973.[199] As the Supreme Court noted in *Roe v. Wade*, "In the past several years . . . a trend toward liberalization of abortion statutes has resulted in adoption, by about one-third of the States, of less stringent laws, most of them patterned after the ALI Model Penal Code."[200] In a footnote, the court pointed out that four states (Alaska, Hawaii, New York, and Washington) had repealed criminal penalties for abortions performed in early pregnancy.[201] Thus a pattern similar to the present one in Western Europe was emerging in the United States.

If the issue were returned to the states today, it therefore seems likely that a very few states might return to strict abortion laws, a few more would endorse early abortion on demand, and the great majority would move to a position like that of the typical middle range of European countries, reflecting popular sentiment that early abortions should be treated more leniently, but that all abortion is a serious matter. The American experience with strict and easy divorce up to the reforms of the 1960s indicates that if abortion law were left up to the states, the number of strict states would be very small. Where strict abortion law or practice coexists in geographical proximity to a system with lenient law or practice, avoidance of the stricter system by travel is an easy matter for those who can afford it. This has been the case in Australia, where the abortion law of the "deep North" states is relatively restrictive, and in Switzerland, where some cantons interpret the defense of necessity much more narrowly than others.[202] Another reason for thinking the strict position would be rare is that compromise legislation in Western Europe has remained fairly stable, while the strict position has eroded, as illustrated most dramatically by the movement in Portugal (1984) and Spain (1985) from very restrictive to compromise legislation. The pressure thus appears to be toward conformity with the dominant pattern. This pattern is apt to be reinforced by the development and use of self-administered prescription drugs to induce early abortions. If abortion in the first few weeks of pregnancy becomes a matter of controlled substances, it will be practically impossible to regulate, since the same substances will be prescribed for preventing pregnancy as for terminating it.[203]

Abortion as a Women's Issue

At this point, however, a worrisome question arises about official regulation of abortion. Must not even the most ardent opponent of abortion feel somewhat uncomfortable about the fact that the basic policy decisions concerning abortion are made by legislatures and courts which are composed overwhelmingly of men? Ruth Ginsburg and Laurence Tribe are right to emphasize, as the U.S. Supreme Court in *Roe v. Wade* did not, the aspect of abortion as a women's issue.[204] It is often overlooked that *Roe v. Wade* and later abortion decisions, such as *Colautti v. Franklin,* and *Thornburgh v. American College of Obstetricians and Gynecologists,* are, in important ways, decisions about doctors' rights as much as they are about women's rights.[205] There is something disturbing about the thought that persons who have never been, and never will be, in the situation of a woman confronted with an unwanted pregnancy are telling that woman what she may or may not do about it. It is so easy to intimidate the frightened and helpless, especially when one can claim to do so on behalf of those who are even more helpless—and not terribly hard to take a lofty moral position when it costs us nothing.[206]

Do we have any idea of how a more truly representative legislature might approach the question of abortion? The answer is by no means obvious. Women have taken the lead on both sides of the question. Men have obvious interests that are served by easy access to abortion. Some recent contributions to the theory of moral development have suggested that women may have "different ideas about human development, different ways of imagining the human condition, and different notions of what is of value in life" from those generally held by men.[207] The psychologist Carol Gilligan believes her research shows that women tend to construct moral problems as problems of responsibility and relationships rather than rights and rules.[208] Another way of putting the point is that while men's moral universe tends to be constructed around what you should *not* do to others, women's tends to be constructed around what you *should* do for others.[209] This, it is claimed, fits with women's heightened sense of life as a web, of connectedness and relatedness, as contrasted with men's sense of self and autonomy, and of life as a hierarchy.[210] (Those who claim that these dichotomies are extensively gender-related in our own society do not, of course, suggest that they are inherently so, or that all men and women conform to these ideal-types.)[211]

If it is true that women in general do "perceive and construe social reality differently from men," the inclusion of women's experience might indeed be expected "to change basic constructs of interpretation."[212] With such notions in mind, Kenneth Karst set himself the task of trying to figure out what the consequences would be of "a reconstruction of our constitutional law to include an important measure of that distinctive morality and worldview."[213] Asserting that "No lawyer can think about these contrasting moralities without being struck by their relevance to the way we think about law," Karst defends the idea of "a constitutional law that takes into account a view of life, self, and morality that is the dominant mode among the female half of the nation's population"; that is, "a view of justice that sees values not merely in autonomy but in interdependence and care about real harms to real people."[214]

Although Karst—curiously—does not discuss *Roe v. Wade,* the lens he holds up to our eyes makes *Roe,* with its emphasis on the separateness, the rights, and the self-determination of individual women look like a very "masculine" decision, while the West German Constitutional Court's opinion, with its emphasis on responsibility for others, and on the social bonds of the community as well as individual rights, seems more reflective of what Gilligan and others have identified as feminine values. It is interesting in this connection that more women than men approved the West German decision,[215] and that the strongest supporters of abortion prior to *Roe v. Wade* were affluent white men.[216] Demographer Judith Blake's interpretation of this statistic is that such men, being financially vulnerable, favored abortion because it freed them from responsibility.[217] A kinder explanation, however, in line with Gilligan's analysis, would be that this category of males was expressing its empathy with women in the way that

51

seemed most natural to them—in terms of individual self-determination.

Though *Roe* could thus be regarded as a "masculine" decision, I do not believe that would be an adequate or accurate interpretation. The voice that we hear in the Supreme Court's abortion narrative—presenting us with the image of the pregnant woman as autonomous, separate, and distinct from the father of the unborn child (and from her parents if she is a minor), and insulated from the larger society which is not permitted even to try to dissuade her or ask her to wait to get counseling, information, or assistance—is more distinctively American than it is masculine in its lonely individualism and libertarianism.

Whatever else they may mean, the abortion cases do not easily lend themselves to the interpretation that the uniqueness of American abortion law consists in protecting women against sexual and economic oppression better than other countries do. The privacy concept in this area is profoundly ambiguous. On the one hand, it gives women freedom of choice concerning abortion, but on the other hand, as Catharine MacKinnon has pointed out, the wall of privacy around sex and reproduction leaves women unprotected in areas where men are arguably still dominant.[218] Deregulation of abortion, among other things, makes it simpler for men to decline to assume responsibility for children. In this connection, it is striking how many of Carol Gilligan's subjects in her chapter on the abortion decision stated that one of the reasons they were seeking abortions was because the men in their lives were unwilling to give them moral and material support in continuing with pregnancy and childbirth.[219] This fact surely must have been central to their moral dilemma, but Gilligan, surprisingly, never picks up on this aspect of her data.

Thus it seems a re-examination of *Roe v. Wade* would not necessarily represent a setback for women. However, if we view abortion within the broader context of laws relating to economic dependency, European comparisons suggest that legislation, while according increased protection to fetal life, could also do much more than American law does at present to advance important interests of women.

Abortion and Dependency

If we do one day rethink our entire public policy relating to abortion, some aspects of the European experience are, I would submit, particularly important for us to take into account. Abortion regulation as such should be viewed in the context of other laws relating to mothers and children. If we are to move from abortion on demand to reimposition of restrictions on abortions in certain situations, we should review the entire complex of laws that bear on maternity and child-raising, including but not limited to our welfare and child support laws. An important segment of the prolife movement has already recognized that those who would restrict or deny abortion should be prepared to give the pregnant woman every possible form of assistance. If the state is once again to restrict the availability of abortion and to affirm the value of unborn life, it should in all fairness strive to help those who bear and raise children, not only during pregnancy but also after childbirth.

At present we lead the developed world in our extreme liberty of abortion, while we lag behind the countries to which we most often compare ourselves in the benefits and services we provide to mothers and to poor families, and in the imposition and collection of child support obligations. The European experience leads one to wonder why pregnant women in the United States should be asked to make significant sacrifices (whether they abort or bear children), if absent fathers and the community as a whole are not asked to sacrifice too. As Kamerman and Kahn have shown in their extensive cross-national studies, the United States is far behind most industrialized countries in the provision of family benefits and services.[220] Here I can only summarize some of their major findings, but even a brief account suggests how importantly these factors might influence an individual woman's decision about whether or not to seek an abortion. It is obvious, too, that these programs tell us a good deal about the attitudes in various countries toward the human resources represented by their future citizens.

First, let us consider maternity leaves. In the United States paid maternity leaves are not required by federal law, and are in practice available only to a minority of working women. When they are available under state law, employer policy, or collective bargaining agreement, they are usually brief, about six to eight weeks.[221] In contrast, most European countries by law assure an employed pregnant woman a paid maternity leave of six months.[222] In Sweden the leave extends to nine months and may be shared between mother and father.[223] The total package of maternity benefits in these countries typically includes medical care during pregnancy and at the time of childbirth. After the paid maternity leave has been used up, many of these countries give mothers the right to an additional year of unpaid leave, with full job protection and fringe benefits.[224] In addition, parents in many countries are guaranteed a certain number of days of paid leave each year for care of a sick child.

A second contrast with the United States is that most European countries provide day care for children ages three to five within the public educational system.[225] In the United States child care may be sponsored or subsidized by some employers, chiefly the larger firms, and, like maternity leave, tends to be available mainly to full-time women workers with good jobs. And third, except for the United States, every one of the fourteen industrialized countries Kamerman and Kahn studied provides all families with children a cash grant whose purpose is to assist with the financial burdens of child rearing.[226] These grants are in varying amounts, but in some countries, such as France and Sweden, they represent very significant additions to the income of poor families, whether one- or two-parent.[227] These cash supplements are typically combined with favorable treatment for families in the tax system. The United States makes no direct allowances to families with children; AFDC allowances are in most states insufficient to take poor families past the poverty level, and the tax benefit system has little value to those poor families who most need assistance.

In countries that offer special support for mothers around the time of childbirth, substantial income supplements to families with children, extensive public health services, and public child care, one might expect the abortion decision to appear in a somewhat different light than it would to a woman in a country that does not provide such extensive income redistribution in favor of families with dependent children. In 1981 Kamerman and Kahn concluded a comparative study of the family benefit-services packages of France, East and West Germany, Sweden, Hungary, and the United States, with the observation: "It is difficult to believe that the United States, which ranks low or last on much child care provision and in all family social benefits, can continue to ignore the consequences for society at large."[228] Against this background, what seems most troubling about the American abortion-funding cases[229] is not so much that they discriminate between poor and middle-class women, but that their total legal context discourages pregnant poor women, single or married, *both* from continuing with the pregnancy *and* from getting abortions.

A Martian trying to infer our culture's attitude toward children from our abortion and social welfare laws might think we had deliberately decided to solve the problem of children in poverty by choosing to abort them rather than to support them with tax dollars. I would like to think the Martian would be mistaken. But many Americans do believe that generous child allowances, such as those available in many European countries, would raise the birth rate, especially the rate of births outside of marriage. As it happens, this has not been the case in other countries. In fact, generous child allowances are characteristic of countries with very low birth rates such as Sweden and East Germany.[230] The experience of these smaller and more homogeneous countries may not, however, be a reliable indicator of what our own situation would be in this respect.

In trying to understand why pro-life sentiment, which undoubtedly exists on a wide scale in this country, does not translate into pro-child sentiment when nearly a quarter of all American children under six are poor,[231] we come face to face with an American problem of at least equal magnitude with the abortion question, one that seems to be peculiarly our own and related to our attitudes about race. Abortion cannot be disentangled from larger issues of social justice. It is likely that our laws and attitudes on abortion are affected by the belief that poor children and their families, many of whom are members of racial and ethnic minority groups, are undeserving of assistance. Perhaps we have not wholly escaped from the Spencerian ethics of the nineteenth century, which played a larger role in the Anglo-Saxon world than on the Continent. After the Supreme Court held that abortions need not be publicly funded, many states, especially those with large welfare populations, decided to pay for abortions anyway.[232] Yet no state has significantly raised its level of support to families with dependent children, and disparities among the states are very great—with some states providing benefits to dependent children that rank among the lowest in the developed world.

It is hard to say to what extent the low standing of the United States in comparison with other developed countries with respect to public family benefits and services is related to the fact that the United States, unlike most other nations, has no explicit family policy. Gilbert Steiner downplays the importance of having a national family policy, pointing out that the crucial policy questions really involve priorities accorded to various goals, and that the family policy of most countries seems to be either a hodge-podge of conflicting aims or, upon closer examination, a population policy, a sexual equality policy, or a labor policy. This criticism seems to miss the mark, however, in an important way. It is true that many European countries are officially committed to the pursuit of goals which are not easily reconciled with one another, or have given a priority to one goal which involves some sacrifice of the others. The West German Constitution, for example, provides that "Marriage and the family enjoy the special protection of the State," and, at the same time, that each individual has the right "to the free development of his personality" and that "men and women have equal rights." But the message is not thereby incoherent. The fact that not all of these important values can be fully implemented simultaneously is no reason to decide not to make an official commitment to pursue all of them. It is standard in most European countries to have programmatic rights to the elements of minimum decent subsistence in laws and constitutions, constitutional commitments to the protection of mothers and children, ministries of family affairs in the government, and private voluntary associations to promote the interests of families at the local, national, and international levels. Measured in terms of the significant public assistance available to families in these countries, family policy does indeed seem to make a difference.

The existence of official family policy in European countries seems to have played a role, too, in shaping another highly important element of the legal context of abortion regulation. In the United States the problem of child support (for children born inside or outside of legal marriage) has long been a national scandal. The problems of ascertaining paternity of children born outside wedlock, of the low amounts of support awarded, of the difficulty in collecting and enforcing child support awards are well known and of long standing. In contrast, countries like Denmark, Norway, and Sweden have long had mandatory paternity actions that do in fact result in determining paternity for nearly all children born to unmarried mothers. Several countries now use standard formulas and tables for calculating realistic amounts of child support and have extremely efficient collection mechanisms, including direct deduction of child support from the noncustodial parent's wages. Many countries, in addition, have assumed the risk of noncollection of child support by paying a guaranteed public maintenance allowance to the support creditors while the state attempts to collect what is owing from the support debtor.

The international picture shows some curious contrasts. First, in countries where the idea of the social welfare state is strong, primary responsibility for child support is unambiguously fixed on the parents and backed up by extremely efficient collection machinery. In the United States, where public responsibility for needy children is assumed only grudgingly, there has been until recently little effort to impose child support in adequate amounts and to see that it is collected. Second, European abortion law has been heavily influenced by notions of what is reasonable to require from a pregnant woman, and European child support law by notions of what it is reasonable to require from an absent father. American abortion law and, at least until recently, child support law has expected little from either men or women. Third, the ideology of privacy has become a leading motif in American, but not in other countries' treatment of family matters. When applied to the family, the right to be let alone often turns out in practice to be the right to leave others alone—as American women desiring abortions and men unwilling to pay child support have been able to do with relative ease over the past several years. When we consider the totality of regulations bearing on the question of abortion, it appears more clearly than ever how different the United States' position is, even from that of other countries which have elective abortion. Our law stresses autonomy, separation, and isolation in the war of all against all, in contrast to Sweden where the laws emphasize sex equality and social solidarity, West Germany where the message is pro-life and social solidarity, and France where equality, life, and solidarity are all sought to be promoted. The European laws not only tell pregnant women that abortion is a serious matter, they tell fathers that producing a child is serious too, and communicate to both that the welfare of each child is a matter in which the entire society is vitally interested.

INTERPRETIVE AND CONSTITUTIVE
ASPECTS OF ABORTION LAW

In this chapter I have approached a bitterly fought and perhaps unresolvable American legal problem from the point of view suggested by a cultural anthropologist. American and West European abortion laws have been compared here as "ways of imagining the real." Analyzing law as a carrier of meaning, however, cannot be an end in itself. If it is worthwhile at all to engage in this exercise, it is only as a preliminary step to a better understanding of how law, behavior, ideas, and feelings interact and influence one another. American lawyers widely believe that the effectiveness of law depends upon its being supported by normative consensus, and that the principal task of law makers and law reformers is to conform the law to social reality. But if this is so, as Geertz points out, it means that law is most effective where it is least needed and is "wholly marginal to the main disturbances of modern life."[233] Furthermore, the ordinary view of the relation of law and behavior overlooks the fact that law, like other aspects of culture such as religion, art, literature, science, history, and production relations, is an active part of a given society, contributing to making that society what it is and what it will become.

Thus, although I have suggested here that compromise legislation of the type in effect in most European countries would reflect the existing consensus in our own country, I do not argue that the case for adopting such legislation rests completely on the existence of such a consensus. Law itself often assists in the formation of a consensus, by influencing the way people interpret the world around them as well as by communicating that certain values have a privileged place in society. We need only think here of the roles that the equality principle and the enactment of civil rights legislation have played in shaping our moral attitudes about racial discrimination.

At present, as we have seen, what American law about abortion communicates is that fetal "potential life" is outweighed by any interest at all of the pregnant woman until the last trimester. Even then, fetal life need not be protected as a constitutional matter. If a state does decide to regulate abortion at that point, it must still assure that an abortion can be performed if the mother desires it and if a single doctor judges it necessary to preserve her health, broadly construed to include a notion of "well-being."[234] In contrast, all of the West European laws, while permitting abortion on a wide variety of grounds, communicate that fetal life is an important interest of the society and that abortion is not a substitute for birth control.

An inquisitive person, say, a pro-choice friend, may well ask at this point: If in practice abortion is widely available under these alternative sets of legal arrangements, what difference does it make what message they communicate? Do not these compromise laws merely harass women who will eventually get abortions anyway? A pro-life friend may well want to know whether such laws would save any fetuses. Would they not just cheapen life, without any tangible gain? Both of them might demand to be shown statistics on the incidence of abortion. Does it correlate in any way, they might ask, with the "message" of a country's abortion law? Thus confronted, I have to concede that there appears to be no clear correlation. It is true that the United States substantially leads all Western countries in the rate of legal abortions per thousand women of child-bearing age.[235] But one cannot read very much into this, for, in general, strict and lenient abortion laws do not appear to be related in any simple way to abortion rates. The Netherlands, where abortion is only lightly regulated, has the lowest abortion rate of any European country; while Romania, which has one of the strictest abortion laws, has one of the highest rates, much higher than that of the United States.[236]

It seems probable that cultural factors other than law are playing the dominant role here, as Max Rheinstein concluded they did in his study of the relation between marriage stability and strict or lenient divorce laws in various countries.[237] In the case of abortion, a country's sexual mores, the level of education about birth control, and the availability of birth control devices appear to be importantly related to abortion rates. The religious factor does not operate in the way that some might expect, as is evidenced by the significantly higher abortion rate in Italy than in England, Canada, or West Germany.[238]

"So what is all this talk about meaning and message?" my friends on both sides of the abortion issue might ask, becoming impatient. In response, I have to shift to a type of argumentation that may not satisfy either of them. So far as my pro-life friend is concerned, I cannot claim to her that the type of abortion regulation I have been advocating will directly affect the abortion rate, which is her immediate concern. As she probably knows, in the United States over 90 percent of all abortions now take place in the first trimester.[239] And, as we have seen, the kind of compromise statute likely to emerge in American state legislatures would be apt to be broadly permissive toward abortions at that stage of pregnancy. I would point out, though, that sometimes a legal norm, even though it seems ineffective, can help to create a climate of opinion which impedes more extensive violations of the norm. One may think here of speed limits and no-smoking signs. In the long run, this climate might be important in a number of ways already suggested in this chapter. At a minimum, replacing the right to abortion with a compromise should help to replace strident discord with reasoned discussion about the grounds and conditions under which abortion might be permitted.

I would ask her, too, to turn her attention for a moment away from the fetus and the life or potential life it represents. Once, when the great Belgian moral philosopher, Hercule Poirot, was applying his little grey cells in a highly theoretical way to the solution of a shocking crime, his long-time collaborator Hastings protested: "But Poirot, you haven't even mentioned the victim!"

Poirot replied, "My dear Hastings, everyone knows what murder does to the victim, what I am interested in is what it does to the murderer!"[240] Many distinguished thinkers share Poirot's views. Only recently a moral philosophy professor at Oxford, Jonathan Glover, wrote in an article on the morality of abortion:

> The effects of certain kinds of acts, not on those they are done to, but on those who do them, can be of overriding importance . . . [T]he moral claims of late fetuses and of babies are not exhausted by any rights depending on their qualifying as persons. Perhaps they are not persons, and have less of the required self-consciousness than some non-human animals. But we have reasons to do with ourselves rather than them, for not treating them as merely disposable.[241]

Over time, I would say to my pro-life friend, compromise legislation may aid your cause, because it is what goes on in people's hearts and minds that you really care about. The mores, not the law, are the best protection of the weak and dependent. A law which communicates that abortion is a serious moral issue and that the fetus is entitled to protection will have a more beneficial influence on behavior and opinions, even though it permits abortion under some—even many—circumstances, than a law which holds fetal life to be of little or no value and abortion to be a fundamental right. Such a law might, for example, help to reverse the impact that the abortion decisions appear to have had on the debate concerning withholding treatment from newborns with physical or mental defects.[242]

My pro-life friend is still apt to be dissatisfied. She may now point out that it is all very well to emphasize the importance of the mores. But, calling on twentieth-century history, she will point out that the mores can evolve in surprising ways—hostile as well as favorable to the weak and helpless. Again, I will have to concede that this is true. Now, all I can do is to remind her of the belief and hope especially cherished in American society, that the evolution of the mores is not an inexorable historical process in which we are helplessly caught. If we really believe that to a great extent we make ourselves, individually and as a society, what we are, then we have to assume an active role in the democratic process of education and persuasion, only part of which goes on in legislatures.

In a similar vein, I would say to my pro-choice friend, if he is still there: Please consider what a set of legal arrangements that places individual liberty or mere life style over innocent life says about, and may do to, the people and the society that produces them. In the long run, the way in which we name things and imagine them may be decisive for the way we feel and act with respect to them, and for the kind of people we ourselves become. Thoughtful people, like my pro-choice friend, whose position on abortion is dictated primarily by compassion for the pregnant woman, are also likely to be people who are concerned about how we constitute ourselves as a society. They care about the future and the quality of life. Most Americans, if the polls are accurate, do not desire the extreme and isolating version of individual liberty the Supreme Court endorsed in 1973, at the instance of small elites.[243] Although they want abortion to be legally available in some circumstances, they do not wish for themselves, or want to confer upon others, a fundamental right to dispose of developing life.

To return to Geertz, the "stories we tell," "the symbols we deploy," the "visions we project" in our laws contribute to making us what we are as a society. As Geertz puts it, "The primary question for any cultural institution anywhere . . . is whether human beings are going to continue to be able . . . through law, anthropology or anything else to imagine principled lives they can practicably lead."[244] To some people, of course, these sorts of concerns are simply too remote. But most arguments that the Supreme Court should have left the abortion question to the state legislatures seem to rest ultimately on some notion that such deference would have been desirable, because the legislative process, however imperfect, is a major way in which we as a society try to imagine the right way to live. The Supreme Court's abortion decisions have thus been doubly disappointing to the majority of Americans. Not only did the court get the story wrong, but it foreclosed the possibility of working out a better story.

TWO

DIVORCE LAW

A number of striking parallels in abortion and divorce law have developed over the past two decades in Western countries. Most obviously, divorce, like legal abortion, has been made more readily accessible to more people by a broadening of the grounds upon which it may be sought. In both cases, too, the statutory changes of recent years were preceded by a period of widespread evasion of the law through collusion and travel, and of relaxed judicial interpretations of strict statutes. Just as "health" came to include mental health of the pregnant woman in abortion law, "cruelty" came to encompass mental cruelty in the divorce courts. Here and there statutory changes were made to reflect more liberal ideas about divorce, but the wave of legislative change did not begin in earnest until the late 1960s. Once again, England and California led the way. And, as with abortion regulation, distinct patterns soon emerged in the new divorce legislation.

The changes in divorce law were themselves part of a more general process in which the legal posture of the state with respect to the family was undergoing its most fundamental shift since family law had begun to be secularized at the time of the Protestant Reformation. Beginning in the 1960s, movement in Western family law had been characterized, broadly speaking, and in varying degrees, by a withdrawal of much official regulation of marriage: its formation, its legal effects, and its termination.[1] The removal of many legal obstacles to marriage; the effect of new attitudes of tolerance for diversity combined with older policies of nonintervention in the ongoing marriage; and the transformation of marriage itself from a legal relationship terminable only for serious cause to one increasingly terminable at will, amounted to a dejuridification of marriage. This process of deregulation of the formation and dissolution of marriage, and of the relations of the spouses during marriage, was typically accompanied, however—again in varying degrees—by a continued, and sometimes intensified, state interest in the economic and child-related consequences of marriage dissolution.

In previous discussions of these subjects I have emphasized the broad similarities that appear among the family law systems of several Western countries when they are viewed in historical context.[2] What I wish to explore here, however, is how and why divorce law in the United States differs from divorce law in other countries. In this chapter we will see that most American states have gone further than any country except Sweden in making marriage freely terminable, but that the United States has lagged behind several other nations to which we often compare ourselves in dealing with the economic aspects of marriage dissolution.

The process of legislative transformation of divorce law has produced remarkable legal changes in nearly all of the twenty countries whose abortion law we surveyed in Chapter 1. After outlining these briefly, we will look more closely at the ways in which five of these countries (England, France, West Germany, Sweden, and the United States) have reformulated the grounds for divorce and refashioned their laws relating to the economic aftermath of divorce. In this latter area are located the problems which remain most acute in divorce law generally. My investigation does not find in European models any "solution" for these problems, but it does lead to a few modest suggestions for improving the legal treatment of the economic aspects of divorce in the United States. The chapter concludes with reflections on the manner in which divorce law, like abortion law, may enter into the formation of ideas and attitudes.

THE TRANSFORMATION OF DIVORCE LAW

The redefinition of marriage from a relationship that could be legally terminated before the death of one of the spouses only for grave reasons, if at all, to one which is increasingly terminable upon the request of one party did not take place overnight in Western nations. In fact, the revolution in divorce law was already under way well before the period described here, in which legislatures began to change the law on the books. In several of the countries, mutual consent divorce through collusion had been judicially tolerated for many years, and fault grounds had been expanded by judicial interpretation, chiefly by reading cruelty to include mental cruelty. Furthermore, not all divorce legislation prior to the wave of changes in the 1960s and 1970s was exclusively fault-based. A complicated form of mutual consent divorce was available in the original version of the Code Napoleon that had been received in Belgium and Luxembourg, and insanity had long been recognized as a ground in many countries and in some American states. Australia and a few American states even permitted divorce after a period of separation or on grounds of incompatibility as well as on fault grounds. Germany since 1938, and Sweden since 1915, had permitted divorce on the ground that the marriage had "broken down," in addition to fault grounds. But in general, for one spouse to get a divorce when the other was unwilling and had committed no marital offense (in the technical sense of the divorce laws) was difficult and time-consuming, even where legally permitted. When the spouses had reached agreement, as they eventually did in all but a small percentage of cases, fault grounds everywhere were the speedy route to divorce.

By the 1960s consent divorce disguised as fault divorce was a routine legal matter in many countries, and divorce had become a relatively common way of terminating a marriage. It was at about this time that dissatisfaction began to appear in some quarters with the fact that the legal system required an "innocent" spouse to prove that the other spouse had committed one of the marital offenses listed in the statutes—typically, cruelty, adultery, or desertion. The major criticisms leveled at the fault system were that it tended to aggravate and perpetuate bitterness between the spouses, and that the widespread practice of using perjured testimony in collusive divorces promoted disrespect for the legal system. It was argued that no social interest was served by forbidding the legal termination of a dead marriage and the remarriage of the parties.[3]

Discontent with fault-based divorce seems to have been felt more acutely by mental-health professionals and academics than by the citizenry in general. Max Rheinstein, writing in 1972, was nearly alone among family law scholars in declining to condemn the status quo in which strict fault-based divorce laws were maintained on the books, while easy mutual consent divorce was available in practice. This dual approach to divorce was, he said, a "democratic compromise," which had "resulted in the satisfaction of almost everyone concerned."[4] It was one way of accommodating the ideals of a large part of the population with the practices of those who could not live up to those ideals—even when, as is often the case, they supported them in principle.

Arguments against fault divorce became increasingly influential in the 1960s, especially after they were accepted by two highly respected English committees. The Archbishop of Canterbury's Group and the Law Commission both issued reports in 1966 concluding that traditional English divorce law ought to be replaced with a statute that concentrated on the state of the marriage rather than the behavior of the spouses.[5] When a marriage had broken down, the aim of the law, according to the oft-quoted formulation of the Law Commission, should be to enable the legal ties between spouses to be dissolved with "the maximum fairness, and minimum bitterness, distress and humiliation."[6] The Archbishop's Group, while not accepting this role for church law, found that it was "not an improper or unworthy conception for the law of a secular society to uphold."[7] These notions—that society has no special interest in permanently maintaining the legal shell of a marriage that has failed, and that the role of the law in such cases is to manage the dissolution process with the minimum human cost—became the leading ideas of divorce law reform in England and elsewhere.

Between 1969 and 1985 divorce law in nearly every Western country was profoundly altered.[8] Among the most dramatic changes was the introduction of civil divorce in the predominantly Catholic countries of Italy and Spain, and its extension to Catholic marriages in Portugal. Other countries replaced or amended old, strict divorce laws. Most of these laws had been virtually un-changed since the grounds for ecclesiastical separation from bed and board became the basis for the secular institution of divorce. The chief common characteristics of all these changes were the recognition or expansion of nonfault grounds for divorce, and the acceptance or simplification of divorce by mutual consent. When California in 1969 became the first Western jurisdiction com-pletely to eliminate fault grounds for divorce, the move was thought by some to prefigure the direction of reforms in other places. But it soon became clear that the purist approach was not to find wide acceptance. That same year England, too, passed a new divorce law which purported to make divorce available only when a marriage had irretrievably broken down. But since the English statute permitted marriage breakdown to be proved by evidence of traditional marital offenses as well as by mutual con-sent or long separation, it did not really repudiate the old fault system. As it turned out, compromise statutes of the English type (resembling those already in place in Australia, Canada, and New Zealand) became the prevailing new approach to the grounds of divorce.

In our sample group of twenty countries all but a few have chosen to modernize their systems simply by adding a nonfault ground, such as mutual consent, separation, or marriage break-down to the traditional fault grounds. Typically, the breakdown or separation grounds in these statutes are hedged in by various safeguards for dependents and by waiting periods ranging in length from a few months in some American states to several years in many European countries. (See Table 2.) Several of these com-promise statutes, as the table shows, have provisions granting courts the power to deny a unilateral nonfault divorce altogether if legal dissolution of the marriage would involve exceptional un-fairness or hardship for a nonconsenting spouse who has com-mitted no marital offense.

In just four countries—the Netherlands, Sweden, West Ger-many, and nineteen American jurisdictions—fault grounds for di-vorce were eliminated entirely. The abolition of fault divorce in the Netherlands and West Germany is less than complete, how-ever, since in both places the statutes permit considerations of

Table 2. Grounds for Divorce in Nineteen Countries[a]

	Mixed Fault and Nonfault Grounds			Nonfault Grounds Only	
	Required waiting period of more than 1 year for contested unilateral nonfault divorce	Required waiting period of 1 year or less for contested unilateral nonfault divorce	Mutual consent required for nonfault divorce	Judicial discretion to deny contested unilateral divorce	No judicial discretion to deny divorce
	Austria (1978)	Canada (1968–86)	U.S. (2 states)	Netherlands (1971)	Sweden (1973)
	Belgium[b] (1974–82)	Switzerland[b] (1907)		West Germany (1976)	U.S. (18 states and D.C.)
	Denmark (1969)	U.S. (22 states)			
	England[b] (1969)				
	Finland[c] (1929–48)				
	France[b] (1975)				
	Greece (1983)				
	Iceland[b] (1921)				
	Italy (1970–75)				
	Luxembourg[b] (1975–78)				
	Norway (1918)				
	Portugal (1975–77)				
	Spain (1981)				
	U.S. (8 states)				

[a] This table classifies countries according to two criteria: the extent to which their divorce statutes have (1) abandoned the fault principle and (2) accepted the possibility of divorce by one spouse of a partner who opposes the divorce and has committed no marital "fault." The dates of the most recent major changes relating to the grounds of divorce are in parentheses. Countries vary, of course, in the extent to which these ideas are put into practice by the courts, the cost of implementing statutory rights, the opportunities offered for tactical delay, and so on. Ireland, which allows no divorce, is not included in the table.

[b] In these systems of mixed grounds, the court has discretion to deny a divorce sought by one spouse against a nonconsenting partner who has committed no "fault" in the technical sense of the divorce laws.

[c] In 1986, the Finnish government introduced a bill to make marriage dissolution available on nonfault grounds only, with no discretion to deny divorce.

fault to come in through the back door.[9] In both of these countries judges have the power to deny a divorce under certain circumstances, even though the marriage in question can be shown to have broken down.[10] In West Germany, in principle, a three-year period of separation is required before one spouse can terminate a marriage against the will of the other.[11]

By 1985, when South Dakota adopted mixed grounds, not a single country or state in our sample held to the pattern that had earlier represented the majority approach: the system under which divorce was available only as a sanction for the serious failure of one spouse to live up to the minimum legal obligations of marriage. The extremes in the mid-1980s are marked at one end by Ireland, the only divorceless country in this group, where 63 percent of the voters rejected the introduction of divorce in a 1986 referendum. At the other end of the spectrum, Sweden and nineteen American jurisdictions have accepted the idea that each spouse has a right to a divorce. Canada since 1986 and twenty-two American states are very close to this position, because the breakdown ground in their statutes is available after a waiting period of a year or less, and the courts have no discretion to deny a divorce on hardship grounds.[12]

Although all five countries whose law will be used here for illustrative purposes were engaged in a broadly similar process of liberalization of the grounds for divorce, there are significant differences among the statutes that they produced. After examining the differences in the new bases for divorce and the ideology of marriage they express, we will turn to variations in the legal treatment of the practical economic effects of divorce in the same group of countries.

THE MOVE TOWARD FREE
TERMINABILITY OF MARRIAGE

Mixed Grounds

The English Divorce Reform Act of 1969[13] was thought in its day to represent a real innovation because it purported to make irretrievable breakdown of the marriage the sole ground of divorce. However, as already noted, the English statute is really just a variant of the popular mixed-grounds compromise. It provides that breakdown of a marriage can be shown only by proving one or more of five facts, three of which—adultery, desertion and "unreasonable behavior"—involve fault. It did mark a symbolic departure from the previous English system, however, in that it explicitly (but very cautiously) made mutual-consent divorce available after a two-year separation and permitted unilateral non-fault divorce after the spouses had lived apart for at least five years. This latter form of divorce (dubbed "Casanova's Charter" by its opponents) was highly controversial, even though it was accompanied by a "hardship clause" that empowered the court in exceptional cases to dismiss the petition if the court was convinced that dissolution of the marriage would result in "grave financial or other hardship" to the respondent, and that it would "in all the circumstances be wrong" to dissolve the marriage.[14] Thus, in England, a spouse who wants a divorce but does not have fault grounds or the other spouse's consent must wait five years after separation before filing suit, and even then, in a rare case, may fail.[15]

Despite the introduction of mutual consent and separation grounds in the 1969 Act, proof of marriage breakdown through fault remains by far the most popular basis of divorce in England, apparently because divorce on fault grounds is quicker. In 1984 fully 37 percent of divorces were on grounds of "unreasonable behavior" and 30 percent on grounds of adultery; only 24 percent involved mutual consent after two years' separation.[16] A mere seven percent were granted on petitions after five years of separation. The old-style disguised consent divorce is thus still thriving in England.

Although some believe that Parliament will eventually eliminate fault completely as a way of proving marriage breakdown, perhaps by requiring one year's separation instead, this did not happen in the 1984 revision of English divorce law.[17] The major change that has taken place in English divorce law since 1969 was the introduction in the 1970s, by court rule, of a procedure under which the parties in uncontested cases need not appear in court. In these "postal divorce" cases, a registrar now merely reviews and certifies the parties' affidavits and forwards their file to the judge for automatic issuance of a decree. Since nearly all (98 percent) of English divorce cases are undefended by the time of the final decree, this simple procedural change has in effect converted divorce in England from a regular lawsuit to a summary administrative procedure.[18] The routinization of divorce that has taken place in this way obviously results in a great discrepancy between the practice and the statute—which still imposes the duty on the court to inquire into the facts of each case to see whether the marriage has really broken down. In retrospect, therefore, a cost-cutting procedural change, effected without fanfare, seems to have had a much greater impact on divorce in England than the much-discussed and widely publicized 1969 Act.

The English Divorce Reform Act of 1969 and the French Divorce Reform Law of 1975[19] show many superficial similarities so far as the grounds of divorce are concerned. France, too, replaced a system under which marriage had been terminable only for serious cause with a new system of mixed grounds. Like England, it innovated by adding mutual consent divorce and a form of unilateral divorce that was controversial even though it is available only after a long separation. In France, as in England, fault grounds are still the most widely used, but by a much narrower margin. The mutual consent ground (which is presented in the statute as the preferred form of divorce) figures in nearly half of all French divorces, while the unilateral nonfault ground is used in only one percent.[20]

In preparation for the 1975 reform in France, behavior and opinion studies of unprecedented scope were carried out. They recorded a wide variety of views and practices with respect to marriage and divorce. The draftsman of the reform law, Jean Carbonnier, interpreted the studies as revealing not only divisions among different groups in French society, but an ambivalence in the hearts of individual French men and women.[21] Feeling that this lack of consensus ruled out a monolithic approach, he drafted a law which maintains the ideal of marriage as a life-long union for better or worse, but which recognizes that the ideal is not universally shared or realized. As in England, the statute does not give one spouse an absolute right to divorce an unwilling "innocent" partner, even after the couple has been separated for a long time. Carbonnier has written that in France this would have been widely considered to be "divorce by repudiation . . . a tragedy for the wife and an object of horror in our Western societies."[22] Thus he included a hardship clause in the new sections permitting unilateral nonfault divorce. Divorce may be sought by one spouse on the ground of "prolonged disruption of the life in common," which can be proved by showing either that the spouses have been separated for six years or that the marriage has been disrupted for six years by the mental illness of a spouse.[23] But a petition for divorce on this ground may be dismissed if it is established that the divorce would entail "material or moral consequences of exceptional hardship" for the unwilling spouse or for the couple's children.[24]

Although the English and French grounds for divorce and their hardship clauses are broadly similar, their effects in practice are somewhat different. In England the courts hardly ever deny a divorce on the basis of hardship, while French lower courts, especially in the provinces, have accepted the defense in a small but significant number of cases.[25] Furthermore, in England "hardship" has been given a strictly economic interpretation (the rare cases have been mainly concerned with loss of pension rights), whereas French courts which accept the hardship defense frequently have done so on the so-called "moral" grounds, usually having to do with the supposed effect of divorce on the nonconsenting spouse's physical or mental health.[26] The highest French court for civil matters, the Court of Cassation, has held that what amounts to exceptional hardship is a question of fact in each case, and thus within the "sovereign power of appreciation of the trier of fact."[27] This means that considerable regional variation in results will be tolerated. For example, in 1984 a trial court in Perpignan (near the Spanish border) dismissed a husband's petition for divorce because it appeared that the wife, "who suffers already from having been abandoned by her husband, would be subject to reproach within her customary milieu (a Catholic community) by reason of the granting of a divorce, even though it would not have been based on [her] fault."[28] Other French courts have denied divorces for such reasons as that the defendant-wife was "beyond reproach," or that she had "run the household and raised six children," or that "she had lost three children and had then been subjected to the indignity of seeing her husband turn to another woman."[29] The French provincial courts seem, without statutory authority, to be applying a test like the one that is written into the English statute but largely ignored by English judges: they deny the divorce if it appears to them that it would "in all the circumstances be wrong." They seem quite unconcerned that the harm complained of is usually not caused by the legal event of divorce but the fact of separation. The Paris courts, on the other hand, interpret the hardship clause quite restrictively.[30] Their interpretation, which has the approval of most French family law scholars, seems to be gaining ground.

Another difference from England is that France has not moved nearly so far toward making divorce a summary procedure. Indeed, the 1975 French law in certain ways made divorce more complicated than it was under the old fault system. It introduced several procedural steps meant to safeguard the interests of the weaker party, and, as we shall see, a rigorous new system of rules governing the financial consequences of divorce.

A year after France revised its divorce law, West Germany enacted a statute which went a step further than either France or England had taken. The thirty-eight-year-old divorce law which was in effect in West Germany on the eve of the 1976 reforms resembled in many respects the new statutes adopted in England in 1969 and France in 1975. It provided for divorce on a variety of fault and nonfault grounds, including marriage breakdown if the spouses had been separated for three years.[31] Like the English and French laws, the 1938 German law specified that divorce on the breakdown ground could be denied if special circumstances would make it unjust in a given case. The innovation of the 1976 divorce reform law was to replace all the specific grounds for divorce with a single nonfault ground: the failure of the marriage, which is irrebuttably presumed if the spouses have lived apart for one year and both consent to the divorce; or, regardless of consent, if the spouses have lived apart for three years.[32] Marital misconduct is supposed to be irrelevant except when the parties have been separated for less than a year.[33]

The 1976 West German law contained a hardship clause, permitting the judge to deny a divorce if the continuation of the legal existence of the marriage was found to be "exceptionally necessary" in the interest of minor children of the marriage, or if dissolution of the marriage would impose severe hardship on the unwilling spouse.[34] But unlike the English and French hardship clauses, the West German one, as originally enacted, could not be invoked after the parties had lived apart for more than five years. This absolute outer limit of five years made the West German reform statute ideologically quite different from the English and French divorce laws. In 1981, however, the Federal Constitutional Court ruled that this five-year cutoff was unconstitutional under Article 6 of the West German Basic Law, which provides that "Marriage and the family are under the special protection of the state." The court held that, even after five years' separation, a spouse opposed to a divorce must at least be given an opportunity to try to prove that a divorce decree would produce extraordinary hardship for him or her.[35] In 1986 the legislature repealed the unconstitutional five-year limit and let the original hardship clause stand. This retrenchment from recognizing a right to divorce has had few practical consequences, however. As of 1983, there had been only sixteen published decisions dealing with the question, and divorces had been denied in only two of these.[36]

So far, then, we have seen that the divorce laws presently in effect in England, France, and West Germany permit one spouse to divorce an unwilling and legally guiltless partner, after a period of separation of five, six, and three years respectively, but keep open the possibility that the court may dismiss the petition in such cases if the divorce would cause exceptional hardship. In practice, hardship clauses are rarely applied to deny a divorce in England and West Germany, but the clause is occasionally used to deny divorces in some parts of France.

Like compromise statutes on abortion, mixed-grounds divorce statutes are hard to justify in theory. To many people, admitting the breakdown principle seems entirely incompatible with the retention of fault grounds. But there are good practical reasons why most countries have rejected exclusive breakdown grounds, or have qualified them as did West Germany and the Netherlands. Pure nonfault grounds with a short waiting period make unilateral divorce available virtually on demand, which is still politically unacceptable in most Western countries. On the other hand, pure nonfault grounds with long waiting periods (the approach proposed by the Irish government in the spring of 1986) would not respond to the perceived need to permit people whose marriages have failed to get on with their lives, a need which gave rise to the demand for liberalized divorce in the first place.

Mixed grounds are a rough-and-ready accommodation of the desire to wind up dead marriages without appearing to endorse the view of marriage as existing only for individual self-fulfillment. Relatively quick divorce is available on fault grounds once the spouses have come to terms about money and children. But mixed grounds give a nonconsenting and "innocent" spouse a period of years (sometimes quite long) during which he or she is entitled to whatever psychic comfort or material benefit the mere fact of being legally married can afford, while denying a license to remarry to the other partner. This may be as hard to defend logically as the term solution in abortion law, but it seems to respond in a similar way to a widespread popular sense of how to deal with a difficult social problem that has no good solution. Now we turn to two variants of a quite different model.

Divorce on Demand

In Sweden liberalization of the grounds for divorce has been taken further than in any of the other countries in our sample except for some of the American states. In 1973 Sweden replaced a system of mixed fault and nonfault grounds with a system which permits either spouse to terminate a marriage without having to allege and prove fault, without having to obtain the other spouse's consent, and without a long period of separation. The petitioner need not even give a reason such as that the marriage has irretrievably broken down.[37] If one spouse desires a divorce, he or she need only petition for one. If the other spouse opposes the petition, or if there are children under sixteen, a six-month "period of consideration" must be observed. After that, the courts are given no discretion to deny a divorce on hardship or any other grounds. If the spouses have already been separated for at least two years, no waiting period need be observed.

The principles behind the Swedish legislation were made explicit at various stages of the legislative process. The then minister of justice instructed the committee drafting the 1973 law that "legislation should not under any circumstance force a person to continue to live under a marriage from which he wishes to free himself."[38] The drafting committee, in presenting the new law, stated that the statute was meant to establish that "not only entry into marriage, but also its continued existence, should be based on the free will of the spouses" and that "the wish of one of the spouses to dissolve the marriage should always be respected."[39] In 1986 the Finnish government introduced a bill to modernize its nearly sixty-year-old divorce legislation along Swedish lines.

The United States, as would be expected of a federal system which leaves domestic relations largely to be governed by state law, exhibits considerable variation from state to state in the details of divorce law. However, the tilt is decidedly toward easy nonfault divorce. As Table 2 shows, the great majority of countries in our sample permit nonfault divorce over the opposition of one spouse only after a rather lengthy period of separation. Most American jurisdictions (forty states and the District of Columbia), by contrast, require a year's separation or less for such a divorce. No state has anything resembling the hardship clause commonly found in West European divorce statutes. The defense of recrimination once operated as a crude functional equivalent of a hardship clause. But in the United States, unlike the Netherlands, the introduction of nonfault grounds was thought to rule out the possibility of denying a divorce to a spouse who was found to have been predominantly responsible for the breakdown of the marriage.[40] Only two American states, Mississippi and New York, seem to limit the use of the breakdown grounds to those cases where both spouses consent.[41]

The reasons for the drift toward easy divorce in the United States are fairly obvious. American experience under the old fault system showed that by the 1960s our courts were for the most part unwilling, or lacking in time, to inquire into the respective grievances of the spouses. Fault divorce had thus already been substantially converted in practice into nonfault mutual consent divorce. In the small number of cases where one spouse remained firmly opposed to the divorce, the existence of a few lenient jurisdictions made divorce and remarriage possible for a determined spouse with the mobility and means to secure a decree in another jurisdiction. As the number of states where divorce was readily available increased, it became harder and harder for any given state to maintain a significantly more restrictive policy than its neighbors.

It is interesting to note, however, that in the United States, unlike in Sweden, ideas of individual liberty did not play a major role in the process of law reform. Herma Hill Kay, who played an active role not only in California's divorce reform but also in the drafting of the Uniform Marriage and Divorce Act of 1970, wrote in 1972 that the original proposals in both cases had rested "upon notions of family privacy: namely, that married persons ought to have the right to terminate their relationship just as they had the right to begin it, subject only to the law's power to insist that the custody and support of their children be provided for adequately and that their financial affairs be settled equitably."[42] If such thoughts were in the minds of the draftsmen, however, they concealed them well. When a California Governor's Commission first recommended in 1966 that fault grounds for divorce be completely eliminated, its report stated:

> We believe that it is personally tragic and socially destructive that the Court should be absolutely required, upon proof of a single act of adultery or "extreme cruelty"—perhaps regretted as soon as committed—to end a marriage which may yet contain a spark of life . . . The marriage relationship is a deep and complex one, and should not be sundered by the law unless the Court finds that the legitimate objects of the marriage have been irretrievably lost.[43]

In a similar vein, the draftsmen's comments to the Uniform Marriage and Divorce Act of 1970 insist that there is to be a real inquest into the fact of marriage breakdown in each case.[44] The provision establishing "pure" nonfault grounds for divorce is described in the comments as giving to judges "discretion to weigh all the evidence bearing upon the death of the marriage."[45] At the time, no one seems to have pointed out that busy judges with crowded dockets would probably give no more attention to the circumstances under which a marriage had allegedly broken down than they were currently giving to tales of "cruel and abusive treatment." Predictably, under the new laws, inquest into the reality of breakdown became a mere ritual.

After California broke the ice in 1969, breakdown grounds caught on quickly. Within sixteen years, *all* American states had fallen in with the trend—many by following California, but more by adding nonfault to traditional grounds. In contrast to most West European systems, however, the American nonfault grounds were not accompanied by strict safeguards. Yet unlike Sweden, most American states still require the statement of a reason (even if it is only "irretrievable breakdown" of the marriage) and preserve at least the form of a judicial inquest into whether the marriage has in fact broken down.

Ironically, American law—apparently without any particular purpose to do so—has taken the idea of individual freedom to terminate a marriage even further than has Swedish law, in three ways. In the first place, as we shall see in the following section, it is less certain in the United States than in Sweden and other continental countries that a former breadwinner will continue to shoulder substantial economic responsibility for the needs of dependents after divorce. Second, the United States Supreme Court has come close in *Boddie v. Connecticut* to sanctioning a constitutional right to divorce,[46] and in *Zablocki v. Redhail* to establishing a constitutional right to marry successively as many spouses as one wishes.[47] Third, by a curious accident of language, it was in the United States that the new forms of divorce on grounds such as breakdown of the marriage first became popularly known as "no-fault" divorce. In the mixed grounds systems of England and France, what Americans call no-fault divorce is known respectively as divorce on separation grounds and *divorce-faillite* (failure). Even in Sweden and West Germany, where all fault grounds for divorce have been eliminated, terms like "no-fault" divorce are not part of popular speech.

The no-fault idea is so much a part of current American thinking about divorce that it takes some effort now to recall that the shift to breakdown grounds was not promoted or put into effect here on the basis of the notion that no one is at fault when a marriage breaks down. The alleged problem with divorce on fault grounds was not that fault was regarded as always irrelevant to the question of marriage termination. On the contrary, the 1966 Report of the California Governor's Commission on the Family, after recommending the elimination of fault in favor of breakdown grounds for divorce, stated: "We would underscore that this is *not* to say that we think immoral or reprehensible conduct should be overlooked. Quite the contrary, the purpose of adopting the standard we suggest would be to permit, indeed to require, the Court to inquire into the whole picture of the marriage. Misconduct would thus be completely relevant, and could be completely explored."[48]

The legal categories of adultery, cruelty, and desertion were represented as too crude and superficial to deal with the infinite variety of ways in which people in a close relationship can do harm to each other. Some critics of fault divorce opposed it also because they thought the adversarial litigation process was ill-suited to ascertaining or sorting out the relative degrees of fault of the spouses in a troubled marriage. The system had degenerated into a formal recitation of perjured testimony, leaving acrimony in its wake, and supposedly engendering disrespect for the legal system. Most commentators agreed too that the fault system was inappropriate for marriages that simply failed without blameworthy conduct on either side. Some members of the California Governor's Commission and the group appointed by the National Conference of Commissioners on Uniform State Laws to draft the Uniform Marriage and Divorce Act favored the complete elimination of fault considerations, but few argued publicly for a system that would appear always to relieve everyone of personal responsibility for the collapse of a marriage.

It seems to have been a legal coincidence that caused the move to breakdown grounds to be translated back into ordinary language as "no-fault" divorce. At about the same time that divorce reform was being widely discussed in the United States, another area of law, which affects vast numbers of persons in their everyday lives, was being transformed by the introduction of what has become known as "no-fault" automobile insurance. In the tort area nobody meant to suggest that no one is ever at fault when motor vehicles collide. (And certainly no American believes this.) The idea was simply that it would be more efficient and economical to handle the cost of automobile accidents through insurance than to litigate the question of negligence in each case. According to Jeffrey O'Connell, who pioneered the idea with Robert Keeton, the term "no-fault" was coined by journalists.[49] When bills based on the Keeton-O'Connell automobile insurance plan began to be introduced in state legislatures across the country, newspaper headline writers required a shorthand expression to describe the proposed legal changes; "no-fault" was apparently first used by Massachusetts newspapers when that state was in the process of adopting that scheme. Later, O'Connell says, he and Keeton were advised by colleagues to disavow the term since it had connotations they did not intend. They concluded, however, that the label had become so well entrenched that to try to change it would have been "like trying to change the course of the Mississippi River." Once it was established in tort law, it was practically inevitable that the "no-fault" label should then migrate to the new divorce law, where proposed legal changes were similarly designed to eliminate litigation over issues of fault. The term stuck, contributing to giving American divorce law its own unique cast.

In practice, then, there are many similarities among the divorce laws of the five countries discussed here so far as marriage termination in itself is concerned. Under all of these laws, divorce is readily available when the spouses reach an agreement on all issues, as they eventually do everywhere in the great majority of cases. Given that few divorces are contested to the end, there are two main differences among various sets of divorce grounds: one practical and one ideological. The laws differ both in the amount of leverage they afford to one or the other spouse in making an advantageous settlement, and in the messages they communicate about marriage itself and the rights and duties of husbands and wives. The hardship clauses, for example, in the English, French, and West German statutes rule out the notion that divorce can be viewed in some sense as an individual's "right." This is strongly reinforced by the long separation periods required—five, six, and three years—before one spouse can unilaterally terminate a marriage to a legally "innocent" partner in those countries. Long waiting periods are typically combined with other legal provisions which, as we will see in the following section, can aid a reluctant spouse in extracting better economic terms in exchange for agreement to a quicker divorce on fault grounds. A legal system which requires a spouse to wait for several years to divorce a nonconsenting husband or wife is obviously telling a different story about marriage from that told in a country where a divorce is available on one party's demand in a year or less.

In Sweden and in most American states, where there is no legal obstacle to unilateral divorce on nonfault grounds, a "right" to divorce exists in the popular sense. It is true, as Max Rheinstein pointed out, that the "irretrievable breakdown" ground in the United States theoretically gives a judge the power to deny a divorce in any given case on the ground that, so long as the spouses are still alive, no breakdown can be said to be irretrievable, and no differences irreconcilable.[50] But the virtually universal understanding in practice is that the breakdown of a marriage is irretrievable if one spouse says it is.[51] Thus Sweden, most of the United States, and, since 1986, Canada are set apart from all other countries in our sample by the fact that the forms of divorce they have adopted have altered the legal definition of marriage itself by making it a relationship terminable at will.

ECONOMIC CONSEQUENCES OF DIVORCE

The move toward free terminability of marriage has everywhere been accompanied by revision of the laws governing the economic aspects of divorce.[52] Under the older laws a spouse's financial position upon divorce typically depended in important respects on marital "fault." Negotiation, then as now, was the principal mechanism for settling disputes about property division, spousal support, child support, and the related issue of child custody. But so long as divorce was available only on fault grounds, the system could give a considerable bargaining advantage to a legally innocent spouse whose partner was impatient to get a divorce.

Negotiating practices developed in which one spouse might exchange cooperation in obtaining a divorce for economic concessions from the other. In this way, the fault-based systems could and often did operate so as to afford some economic protection to a dependent wife and children when a family broke up. But they also could operate to her detriment if she had committed a marital offense. To the extent that the new divorce laws made it possible or even easy for one spouse to obtain a divorce in spite of the opposition of the other, and made fault less relevant or even irrelevant to property and support issues, the dynamics of bargaining over finances were significantly altered. Reformers soon realized that changes in the grounds of divorce would require a reformulation of the laws governing property division, alimony, and child support.

So far as the principles on which reforms in these areas should be based were concerned, the following statement of the Archbishop of Canterbury's Group expressed sentiments widely shared twenty years ago in Europe (and also shows how far removed the "breakdown" concept was from the idea of "no fault"): "it would be intolerable to allow the party responsible for breakdown to petition [for divorce] so long as the economic and financial rights of the other party, together with the rights of any children of the marriage, were not fully protected, and our recommendation of the principle of breakdown is therefore conditional on that protection being assured."[53] Under the influence of this kind of thinking, the legal regulation of the economic aspects of divorce began to be re-examined.

In continental Europe two basic models emerged. The predominant model retains considerations of fault and emphasizes the financial obligations of the former provider, supplemented where necessary by the state. This first model is typical of the Romano-Germanic legal systems. The second is the Nordic model, which minimizes the role of fault and places more emphasis on spousal self-sufficiency combined with "realistic" child support obligations and strong programs of public benefits for families with children. Whichever model they more closely resemble, most continental European systems have this in common: child support is calculated according to formulas or tables in a relatively predictable fashion, and community property in principle is divided equally unless the spouses have made some other arrangement by marriage contract or divorce settlement. Both continental patterns are legally differentiated from the third model, the Anglo-American, primarily by the extensive discretion English and American statutes accord to judges in reallocating the spouses' property and in assessing support obligations, and by the large measure of freedom English and American spouses have to make their own financial arrangements, even concerning child support.

The three models differ from one another in the way they allocate financial responsibility for minor children after divorce among the custodial and noncustodial parents, and society as a whole. But the differences are nuanced. Custodial parents everywhere shoulder the main economic burdens of divorce, but in the English and American systems they receive less direct help from the state than in the Nordic group, and less help in enforcing the obligations of the former principal provider than in either the Nordic or the Romano-Germanic group. The three models will be examined primarily to see how they operate in divorces involving couples with minor children, which in all the countries discussed here constitute the majority of divorce cases.

Continental Models

Countries with Romano-Germanic legal systems typically treat marital fault as a factor that may be considered to some extent in fixing spousal support, and place definite limitations on the spouses' freedom to make their own financial arrangements in connection with divorce.[54] The continued importance of marital fault in this group of countries is well illustrated by recent developments in West Germany, where the legislature, consistently with eliminating fault grounds for divorce, attempted in 1976 to curtail the role of misconduct in maintenance questions. The 1976 law provided that an otherwise valid claim for spousal support could be denied only in certain very limited cases of "gross unfairness," such as where the marriage was of short duration, or the claimant had committed a crime against the obligor-spouse, or the claimant had deliberately brought about his own state of neediness.[55] Court decisions under the statute constantly expanded the category of gross unfairness, however, and eventually a 1986 amendment incorporated the case law. As a result, spousal support (to a spouse who is not engaged in caring for a child of the marriage) can now be denied or curtailed, not only in the above cases, but also if the claimant deliberately undermined important financial interests of the obligor; grossly neglected his duty to contribute to the support of the family for a lengthy period prior to separation; or was responsible for "obvious and serious misconduct" toward the support debtor.[56] The revised section concludes, as before, with a catch-all general clause providing that gross unfairness can also be shown by other facts equal in seriousness to those specifically listed. Thus, ten years after the switch to pure nonfault divorce, fault is firmly re-entrenched as a major factor in maintenance issues in West Germany.

Divorce laws in the Romano-Germanic countries differ from one another in numerous details, but in general it can be said that the same legislation which, in theory, permits freer terminability of marriage in these countries also establishes rules which make it quite difficult for either spouse to rid himself of family economic responsibilities.[57] In fact, the complaint is sometimes heard that under the new systems of divorce it is actually more difficult and expensive to dissolve a marriage than it was before the grounds for divorce were supposedly "liberalized."[58] The law of France may be taken as an example of the seriousness with which one country in this group approaches the economic aspects of divorce. There, since 1975, divorce theoretically puts an end to the support obligation between spouses,[59] and (if the spouses have not contracted out of the community property system) all assets acquired by the gainful activity of the spouses during the marriage are divided equally. But the abolition of the spousal support obligation is more illusory than real. The same article which eliminates the support duty provides that one spouse may be required to make a payment to the other in order "to compensate, so far as possible, for the disparity which the disruption of the marriage creates in the conditions of their respective lives."[60] This "compensatory payment," which is usually made in periodic installments, thus looks very much like spousal support with a new name. Mutual consent divorces can be granted only if a judge has found that the spouses' agreement on the compensatory payment is equitable.[61] In cases where divorce is granted for the fault of one party, the compensatory payment is, in principle, available to the plaintiff but not the defendant, and a successful plaintiff may also recover damages for any "material and moral prejudice" caused by the dissolution of the marriage.[62]

Cases of unilateral nonfault divorce in France are governed by a special and even stricter set of rules concerning finances. The plaintiff who petitions for divorce on the ground of "prolonged disruption of the life in common" must not only wait six years for the divorce, but must assume all the costs of the proceedings, and after the divorce "remains completely bound to the duty of support."[63] Thus, in mutual consent divorces, which make up nearly half of all marriage dissolutions in France, divorce is conditioned on making financial arrangements that satisfy a judge who does not, as in England and the United States, merely rubberstamp the parties' bargain. In fault divorces, additional economic advantages are given to an "innocent" spouse. And in unilateral nonfault divorces the successful plaintiff obtains little more than legal permission to remarry, so completely is he bound to the economic obligations of the old marriage.

In the Nordic model, as exemplified by Sweden and to a lesser degree by the other Nordic countries, marital fault is irrelevant or less relevant to settling the economic affairs of the spouses upon divorce. Community property is equally divided when the marriage comes to an end, but spousal support plays a very limited role.[64] So far as dependent children are concerned, however, the Nordic countries—like those in the Romano-Germanic group— make every effort to ensure that both parents assume a fair share of the cost of their care after divorce. Parents have some latitude to agree on the amount of child support to be paid by the noncustodial parent, but cannot agree on less than a fixed minimum contribution. Sweden, though making marriage as easily terminable as in several American states, fixes primary responsibility for child support on the parents, assesses it through the use of formulas in a consistent way, and backs it up with what is probably the most efficient collection system and the most comprehensive and generous package of benefits for one-parent families in the world.[65]

The Anglo-American Model

English and American laws on the economic aspects of divorce grant far more discretionary power to judges than do the laws of either the Nordic or Romano-Germanic countries. This freedom to reallocate the spouses' property[66] and to assess spousal and child support in the way that seems fair to the judge is typically justified by an alleged need to adapt the law to the unique circumstances of each individual case. In theory, it sounds ideal. But since judges in both England and the United States routinely approve the spouses' agreements on these matters, the chief effect of these large grants of discretion is to deprive the spouses and their legal representatives of any clear principles that could serve as a background for negotiation. As the American and English systems of virtually unfettered judicial discretion work out in practice, the expense of raising children after divorce falls disproportionately heavily on the custodial parent, who in the great majority of the cases is the mother. Study after study has shown that after divorce noncustodial parents typically enjoy a higher standard of living than that of the custodial parent and dependent children, and indeed often higher than they themselves had prior to the divorce.[67] Support payments figure less importantly in meeting the needs of the children than do the mother's earnings and public assistance, which in the United States and England is less generous than in France, Sweden, or West Germany.[68]

Yet nothing in substantive English and American support laws would lead anyone to expect custodial parents to be regularly disadvantaged relative to noncustodial parents. The principles of child support law, which are fairly similar in all modern legal systems, seem clear and forceful in their demands that both parents share, according to their abilities, in meeting the needs of the child. How then do we explain the precipitous drop in living standard typically experienced by children and their custodial parent after divorce, while the noncustodial parent's standard of living typically rises? Why the discrepancy between the story told by the law on the books and the one revealed by the law in action?

In the United States part of the problem seems to be that the amounts of child support awarded by courts and agreed to in settlements are too low, as a rule less than what noncustodial parents can afford, and typically less than half of what it costs to raise a child at a minimally decent level. Why do judges award, and custodial parents agree to, such low amounts? What do lawyers tell their clients about what to expect? The former welfare commissioner of New York City has suggested that some of these results have to do with the attitudes of judges: "Judicial discretion reigns supreme, and, as it is exercised in many areas of the country . . . it reflects a reluctance to impose any significant burden on the absent father to support his children and little interest in reducing the burden on the public treasury represented by the AFDC program."[69] Carol Bruch has pointed out that judges, like most of us, tend to be ignorant of or to greatly underestimate the actual cost of raising a child.[70] She notes that every time a judge overlooks expenses related to a child's needs or underestimates costs involved in child-raising, the burden falls entirely on the custodial parent.

Yet these problems need not be so severe as they are in the United States. In Sweden, West Germany, and many other countries the problems of adequacy and predictability of support awards have been greatly alleviated by the use of realistic formulas or standardized support tables.[71] When the parties know, with reasonable certainty, what level of support a judge will order if the case goes to trial, their agreement will reflect this. And if they know that an agreement for an amount below a fixed minimum, calculated with reference to the needs of the child and the resources of the parents, will not be judicially approved, a large area of controversy simply drops out of divorce cases. It is to be hoped that the 1984 U.S. federal child support legislation, which required the states by October 1987 to establish tables with nonbinding minimum guidelines for child support, will eventually help to educate judges and improve support agreements.[72] But it falls far short of the rigorous European approaches to the problem.

A further difficulty is that child support agreements and awards, typically inadequate when made, fail to keep up with the cost of living and the increasing needs of the child as it grows older. Child support in the United States must be modified, if at all, in a court proceeding, with all the ill will this generates and with all the expense of time and money that it entails. This problem would be greatly alleviated if support awards rose automatically with the cost-of-living index as they do in France, West Germany, Sweden, and several other countries. The burden would then be on the support debtor to petition to show that individual circumstances make the increase unfair in his case, rather than on the custodial parent to go to court every time an increase was needed.

Finally, in the United States, the problems of the low amounts of child support and the lack of principle or consistency in awarding them are compounded by difficulties in the area of enforcement. The obstacles encountered by support creditors when the support debtor defaults, especially if he is located in another state, have often proved practically insurmountable. Getting the initial child support order has too often been only the prelude to a continuing battle between the ex-spouses, with a series of defaults and attempts at collection involving court time, lawyers' fees, and long periods during which arrearages have to be allowed to build up until another enforcement effort is worth the cost involved. With the Child Support Enforcement Amendments of 1984, however, the United States has finally taken a step toward more effective European-style approaches. Federal law now requires the states, as a condition of eligibility for federal AFDC funds, to adopt legislation providing for automatic wage-withholding when there has been a default in child support for a month or more.[73] Automatic withholding is mandatory in all cases involving clients of state enforcement agencies, and will be available in nonwelfare cases if it is provided for in the support decree.

The experience of other countries indicates, however, that even a very efficient support enforcement system has its limits. In Sweden, for example, where a generous child allowance and other public subsidies for families with children mean that the support demands made on the absent parent are relatively modest, there is still a hard core of cases where little or no support can be collected.

About 15 percent of Swedish divorced parents liable for support pay nothing, while 25 percent pay less than 30 percent of what they owe.[74] In all likelihood, there will always be a significant proportion of cases in which private child support cannot or will not play a major role. Nevertheless, leaving these hopeless cases aside, the Swedish record is encouraging about what can be accomplished through automatic wage withholding. In 1975, 60 percent of Swedish support debtors paid over 90 percent of what they owed, with automatic wage deduction used in about 25 percent of all cases.[75]

Thus there is reason to be optimistic about the eventual impact of the 1984 federal child support legislation in the United States, if it is properly implemented at the state level. But even if more adequate amounts of child support come to be awarded here, and even if the states eventually take over much of the burden of collection with new and improved devices for recovering what is owed, important differences will persist between our states and European countries at comparable levels of development so far as the standard of living of children in one-parent families is concerned. These differences have to do with the degree to which the societies in question are willing to redistribute income to families with children. Several continental European governments (including those of France, West Germany, the Nordic countries, Austria, Luxembourg, and many Swiss cantons) not only undertake to collect unpaid child support but also to absorb partially the risk of failing to collect it through what is called the "maintenance advance" system. In these countries, if there is a default in child support payments, all the custodial parent has to do is apply to a public agency. The agency then tries to collect from the noncustodial parent, but in the meantime it advances the amount of child support owed, up to a maximum limit set by law. If the original child support order was for less than this maximum amount, the state makes up the difference, regardless of any default. If the original support order was for more than the maximum maintenance advance, the state not only goes after the debtor to recover what it has advanced, but also, on behalf of the family, to collect the remainder owed.

In addition, in most of these countries a single-parent family receives a package of several other public benefits and services. In Sweden, for example, this package would include free health care, tax benefits, a direct child allowance grant of $600 a year per child, and a housing allowance.[76] If the mother's earnings and child support, plus all these subsidies are insufficient, general social assistance (what we would call welfare) is available. Largely as a result of these differences in the level of public family benefits as well as in private child support, an unmarried, unemployed mother of two in England and the United States lives on half of the net average production worker's wage, while her French, Swedish, or West German counterpart lives on 67 to 94 percent of what an average production worker earns in those countries.[77] In England even this low level of social assistance can be considered generous, given the relatively low per capita gross national product.[78]

The same cannot of course be said for the United States. We tend, *de facto*, to leave the economic problems of female-headed families to the custodial parents themselves, to be solved by their own work outside the home or by remarriage. If custodial mothers are unable to provide for themselves and their children in these ways, we treat their poverty as a welfare problem. Their standard of living then depends on the AFDC support levels set by state law, which, in most states, are too low to bring the recipients' income up to the poverty level, even when combined with in-kind transfers such as food stamps.[79] Some of our difficulties in this area seem to be related to our failure to recognize that Aid to Families with Dependent Children may function quite differently where older, previously married women are concerned than it does in the cases of very young, unmarried mothers. For the former, welfare is usually a temporary aid in making the transition to an independent life, while for the latter, who need more and different kinds of assistance, welfare all by itself may be a trap. We have tended to lump both types of situations together and to try to avoid creating welfare dependency by keeping support levels low. It seems unlikely, however, that higher levels of aid would turn older divorced mothers into welfare dependents. And it may be that poor, young women become trapped in poverty not so much by the availability of welfare as by the perception that society offers them no other role but that of welfare mother.

No country has completely solved the economic problems caused by the breakup of a family, when two households must subsist separately on resources which are usually no greater than they were when the family members were sharing a single home. The modest income and assets of most families, the frequency of marriage dissolution and the formation of new families, the many disadvantages of working single mothers in the job market and the marriage market, and the strained resources of all welfare states make it unlikely that any entirely satisfactory solution to these problems can be found. The situation of a female head of a family with minor children is precarious everywhere. But some countries do more than others to alleviate the burdens of such families and to make sure that they are fairly shared between the former spouses. Countries in the Romano-Germanic legal tradition, especially the poorer countries, typically emphasize the support obligations of the former principal provider. Those in the Nordic group (and some other relatively affluent countries), while strictly enforcing private child support obligations, also characteristically assume a substantial public role in assisting families with dependent children. The United States shows no discernible inclination to increase the public role in the support of such families. Yet our private child support system in practice leaves female-headed families significantly worse off financially than the noncustodial parent. Proceeding on the assumption that the United States will not in the near future greatly increase its level of public assistance to families with children, the following section explores some ways in which private law in the various states might be refashioned so as to improve the circumstances of children after divorce.

SOME PATHS THROUGH THE FOREST

When divorce is viewed as a process of negotiation, two conspicuous flaws appear in American laws relating to its consequences. (At least they are flaws if not carefully restricted to particular classes of cases.) The first is an unusual degree of reliance on judicial discretion, with a resulting lack of certainty about how any given dispute will be decided. This gives an advantage to the spouse who has the time, money, and stamina to wait the other out, or to wear down the other emotionally and economically through costly pretrial discovery and motion practice. Furthermore, several studies indicate that, in exercising their virtually uncontrolled discretion, judges as a rule tend to protect the former husband's standard of living at the expense of ex-wives and children.[80] The essential unpredictability of the system does, of course, permit excesses in the other direction as well. Even though it is not uncommon for a noncustodial parent's child support payments to be lower than his car payments, every support debtor knows someone whose economic circumstances are similar to his, but whose child support payments are lower. Discontent and a sense of the essential unfairness of the system are widespread.

The second weakness in American divorce laws is the failure to provide meaningful supervision or review of agreements between spouses upon divorce. This reliance on private ordering may be appropriate for some kinds of cases, but not where minor children are involved. Such agreements, which constitute in fact the basic mechanism for adjusting disputes about money and children, are hardly ever closely scrutinized, much less set aside by a court. The contrast with both the Romano-Germanic and Nordic models is marked. The continental systems facilitate and structure private negotiation by establishing clear principles and fixed rules, and they provide an independent check at least on whether the interests of any minor children have been adequately protected and secured.

Yet for a number of reasons none of the continental models for dealing with the economic aftermath of divorce would be suitable for the United States. In the first place, each continental country's support and property division law is related in such complex ways to its social welfare law that it is not readily adaptable for use in a system like our own. Second, countries with unitary national legal systems can more easily enforce their marriage and divorce policies than can individual states within the American federal system. Moreover, like the Anglo-American models, they all rest upon a fundamental misconception. Their support and property division laws proceed on the premise that a single set of principles, policies, standards, and rules can and should govern all divorces—

from those involving short, childless marriages, to those involving couples with young children who are still in need of physical care and financial support, to those involving long-term marriages during which children may or may not have been raised and substantial property may or may not have been accumulated. Modern divorce statutes everywhere have established a unitary set of basic rules that treat as exceptional the case that is in fact statistically most frequent—the divorce of couples with minor children.

Improvement of American divorce law must begin with a complete reorientation of the way we presently think about the rules governing the economic consequences of divorce. When almost three-fifths of all divorces in the United States involve couples with minor children,[81] it is astonishing that our spousal support law and marital property law treat that situation as an exception to the general rule. The trend in maintenance law is to emphasize spousal self-sufficiency, by providing in principle no support to a former spouse unless special needs exist.[82] This is because, in theory, discretionary division of marital property is supposed to be the primary mechanism for arranging the spouses' financial affairs upon divorce.[83] Since, however, in the majority of divorce cases one spouse is a custodial parent, special needs are *not* exceptional. They are routinely present. Given the modest assets of most divorcing couples, especially those with young children, the idea of effecting a "clean break" between the spouses through property division is wholly unrealistic in most such cases. They should be subject to a new, separate system of regulation. Just as corporate law has had to distinguish between publicly held and close corporations, and commercial law between merchants' dealings among themselves and their dealings with consumers, it is now time for family law to distinguish between the childless couple and the family with children.[84]

The existence of several kinds of divorces requiring different treatment is presently recognized by the various American states, if at all, only in the form of statutory guidelines and lists of factors to be considered by the court in deciding property and support questions. Typically, state statutes give judges an overall direction to divide property of the spouses in an "equitable" or "just" manner[85] and to award spousal support in cases of need, according to the spouses' respective requirements and resources. When further guidelines are furnished under such statutes, they do not provide a clear and helpful indication of what is "equitable" or of what priorities exist among the various factors enumerated in the guidelines. For example, the law of Massachusetts requires the trial judge to consider no less than fourteen factors (including conduct) and permits him or her to consider two others, in determining what property and support allocation is fair.[86] Nearly all American states now have some variant of these statutes, which are commonly known as "equitable distribution" laws. (This label, which no doubt encouraged their adoption, is something like calling the MX missile a "peacekeeper.") Their authors may have wanted them to raise the level of fairness, but they have great potential to do precisely the opposite.

To extricate ourselves from this situation we need, first of all, to remove from the general divorce law certain categories of cases that call for separate treatment. It would be particularly sensible to separate the two large groups of commonly occurring cases which require quite different approaches: divorces of couples with minor children and terminations of short, childless marriages. For each of these two groups it is not too hard to identify a principle, likely to attract wide support, which could be applied to improve predictability and thus to facilitate fair and expeditious negotiations. The optimal mix of fixed rules and discretion will be quite different in these two situations.

What should a set of special rules for divorces involving couples with minor children look like? The governing principles are already present in our law relating to child support. They merely need to be clarified, extended, and, of course, applied. It is already established that there is a legal duty to provide for the needs of one's minor children, that this duty must be shared fairly between both parents, and that the duty is so important that it cannot be excluded by contract.[87] What has to be made more specific and forceful is that in divorces of couples with minor children, this duty must be given the *foremost* consideration.[88] A "children first" principle should govern all such divorces. It is already implicit in the existing law of child support that the fact of having children engages all of the parents' income and property to the extent necessary to provide for the children, at least until they reach their majority. To apply this principle consistently in divorces involving minor children would mean that the judge's main task would be to piece together, from property and income and in-kind personal care, the best possible package to meet the needs of the children and their physical custodian. Until the welfare of the children had been adequately secured in this way, there would be no question or debate about "marital property." All property, no matter when or how acquired, would be subject to the duty to provide for the children. Nor would there be any question of "spousal support" as distinct from what is allocated to the custodial spouse in his or her capacity as physical custodian. In cases where there is significant income and property left over after the children's needs have been met, the regular system of marital property division and spousal support law could be applied as a residual system.

To a great extent, this is probably what many judges are already trying to do, more or less, in cases that are litigated to the end.[89] But judges who make the attempt are hampered by statutes ill-suited for this purpose, and a federal tax law which in many cases forces mislabeling of what is actually happening, by making it advisable not to call transfers of income or property "child support."[90] Using the legal categories of property division, spousal support, and child support, judges do attempt to put together a package from the spouses' resources to provide for the accommodation and support of the children. But too often they operate in the dark about the actual costs of raising children and with more concern to protect the father's ability to build a new life for himself than for the mother and children whose economic circumstances are likely to be much more difficult. Their starting point seems to be consideration of the father's resources and what they believe he can afford. This contrasts with the continental approach which begins with the needs of child and then turns to whether and to what extent they can be met from the income and property of the noncustodial parent.

Furthermore, one never knows what a particular judge will do in any given case. The perceived arbitrariness of the process must play an important part not only in creating dissatisfaction with the way divorces are handled, but in promoting disillusion with the whole legal system. Prior to no-fault divorce, we heard a great deal about how deplorable it was that the only contact most people had with the legal system was routinely characterized by collusion and perjury. A major argument for moving to objective grounds for divorce was that this would restore respect for the administration of justice. Today, however, far too many divorce litigants feel that the outcomes of cases are simply arbitrary, or dependent on the luck of the judicial draw, or systematically biased.

Yet the most harmful effects of the present system are not those that appear in litigated cases, where judges are often perceived to be acting in an unprincipled or unfair way as they award custody, set support for children and spouses, and reallocate marital property. The greatest damage from the lack of clarity in the law governing such matters occurs in those divorces, the overwhelming majority, which are settled by the parties. These constitute over 90 percent of all divorce cases.[91] It is important that law reform in the area of divorce should respond to the needs of those divorcing couples of modest means for whom the law is a backdrop for the process of negotiation and settlement. Here, and not in the courtroom, is where divorce law has its main impact.

Thus the most important reason for special regulation of divorces involving minor children has to do with the effect a recasting of the law would have on negotiation and settlement in the cases that are never litigated. From the beginning of negotiations, the attention of the parties would be directed toward the present and future needs of their children. They would know that if the economic consequences of their divorce are decided by a court, the judge's main objective will be to arrange their affairs in the best possible way for the children. Most parents will want this too, but present divorce law and tax laws distract them from this one matter upon which they might still be able to agree, and require them to concentrate instead on more inflammatory issues. When cases are settled rather than litigated, and settled early rather than after a series of expensive legal jousts, more assets are preserved for the family members. Reasonable settlements benefit both parties and the children by keeping more property in the pot that will eventually be divided.

A second reason for moving to a special system of rules for divorces involving children is to supply the clear guidelines necessary to assure more predictability and evenhandedness in the minority of cases that are decided by judges. In divorces involving children judicial discretion will always have to play an important role. But with concrete principles to furnish a guide, the case law has a good chance to develop its own internal coherence through the characteristic processes by which the common law has developed in other areas. This in turn will exert a beneficial influence on private ordering after a body of decisions accumulates under the statute.

A third reason is that a system of principles directed toward assuring the continuing welfare of children is much more likely to be accepted by couples caught up in the divorce process than the present system, which is conceptualized almost entirely in terms of the rights and duties of the former spouses toward each other. The perceived legitimacy of the new principle should also have a salutary effect on voluntary compliance with support orders. How we name things has important consequences for how we feel about them and act with respect to them. A recent English study of divorcing couples supports the commonsense notion that fathers are more willing to pay maintenance when they see it as a benefit for their children, rather than an advantage for the former wife.[92] It is highly regrettable that in a recent handbook for lawyers on handling divorce cases, an American divorce court judge must write: "The first question to consider is how the periodic payments from the primary breadwinner to the primary caretaker should be characterized. Although the primary breadwinner may have an emotional aversion to paying 'alimony' and a good feeling about paying 'child support,' the emotional considerations may have serious adverse tax consequences."[93] As the judge, who was himself a long-time family law practitioner, recognizes, it is easier for divorcing spouses to accept that child-begetting involves lasting economic responsibility than that marriage does so.

Law reform proposals regarding support and property disputes between spouses after divorce are always controversial. Some proponents feel that spouses should have continuing economic responsibility for each other after divorce, that marriage should give rise to property sharing, and divorce to property division. Others argue that the mere fact of marriage should not affect title to property or require one ex-spouse to support the other after the marriage has ended. But once children enter the picture, these controversies about spousal rights and duties are, or should be, largely irrelevant. The children-first principle would make this clear.

But to encourage fair and reasonable allocations in settlements, the law must do more than establish that the judge's primary aim is to try to provide for the welfare of minor children. This general principle must be supplemented by subsidiary guidelines. These will involve difficult decisions: What is a "fair" allocation of support duties between mother and father when one provides mainly periodic payments while the other furnishes not only economic support but personal care, thereby incurring disadvantages in the labor market? Is the judge to seek to place the children at minimum subsistence level or at the level of an "average" family; should the judge try to approximate their own former standard of living, to equalize the standard of living of the new family units arising after the divorce, or to let a child participate in the postdivorce standard of living of the wealthier parent? What is the effect of new families on old support relationships? Should there be a minimum child support amount, fixed by a needs-resources formula, which the spouses cannot alter by contract? However these problems are resolved, the resolutions should be in the form of principles applicable to all cases; they should not depend on the reaction of an individual judge to a particular case. The judge's role should be to adapt the principles, not to invent them for each new situation. Ideally, we will move, as European countries have done, and as federal legislation contemplates, to more reliance on formulas or tables.

Is it realistic to think that American divorce law—or divorce law elsewhere—could change in the direction of a children-first principle? A recent English development is highly encouraging. In October 1984 England amended its property division and support guidelines to require judges to give first priority to the welfare of any minor children of the family in making orders for financial provision on divorce.[94] It is too soon to tell whether judges will take this statute as a charter for fundamentally reshaping family finances, or whether they will merely pay it lip service without changing their existing practices. But potentially this statute is of far-reaching significance, especially if it results in property and support awards that more adequately reflect the true cost of maintaining children. The adoption of the priority for children in 1984 just possibly may, like the English divorce law reform in 1969, be the first cautious manifestation of a trend that will take ever bolder forms in other jurisdictions.

The most serious reservation one might have about making the welfare of minor children the central focus of the relevant divorce cases seems to be this: would the change in emphasis in the law increase litigation, or threats of litigation, about fitness for child custody? This is doubtless a grave concern.[95] An American judge has recently given a candid and vivid account of his own use in his lawyering days "of the divorce laws' unpredictability to terrorize women into trading away their support."[96] Justice Richard Neely tells how he once represented a married man who had fallen in love, first with motorcycles and then with a woman who shared his fondness for motorcycles. Even though this king of the road had told Neely that custody of his two children was the last thing in the world he wanted out of his divorce, Neely suggested to him that if he indicated to his wife that he was willing to fight for custody all the way to the state supreme court, the divorce could probably be settled fairly cheaply. The wife, who was unwilling to take any chance, however small, on losing her children, settled on the husband's terms.[97]

Now, as a judge, Neely has become a strong critic of the system that puts child custody up for grabs. The vague and open-ended "best interests of the child" test appears reasonable, he says, "until we understand just how much sinister bargaining is carried on in the shadow of this unpredictable, individual-oriented system."[98] Here, once again, we have an area where unfettered discretion and lack of review of spouses' agreements seems to be a serious problem.

What would be the likely effect of the children-first principle on custody matters? First, there is some reason to believe that the percentage of spouses who will engage in bad faith custody fights will not be increased by a change in the law. In California, when the state switched to divorce on objective grounds and abolished the statutory preference for the mother as custodian of young children, many expected that the change would give rise to an increase in spurious custody litigation. In fact, a study by Weitzman and Dixon showed that after the new law went into effect, the percentage of contested custody cases remained about the same as it was before.[99] If it is true, as the California experience suggests, that people who are disposed to engage in this type of litigation are already doing it on fitness grounds, and that a change in the law is not likely to encourage others to follow suit, the proposed change might actually reduce litigation about custody. To the extent that much existing litigation is the result of personal antagonism between the spouses, any change that diverts the spouses' attention away from their own differences and toward their children's future is apt to be beneficial.

Although the California study indicates that the proportion of spouses who will engage in bad-faith custody challenges is not likely to be *increased* by a change in the divorce law, it does seem clear that the present vague "best interests of the child" test does nothing to discourage, and probably ends up encouraging, custody disputes.[100] The "best interests" standard is an excellent example of the futility of attempting to achieve perfect, individualized justice by reposing discretion in a judge. Its vagueness provides maximum incentive to persons who are inclined to wrangle over custody, and it asks the judge to do what is almost impossible: evaluate the child-caring capacities of a mother and a father at a time when family relations are apt to be most distorted by the stress of separation and the divorce process itself. Robert Burt, pointing out the impossibility of determining what is clearly in the best interests of the child in such circumstances, argues that law reform efforts should concentrate instead on the effect of custody law on private ordering, and has suggested that almost any automatic rule would be an improvement over the present situation.[101]

The currently fashionable concept of joint custody is no panacea, and its virtues seem more illusory than real. Certainly it is desirable to encourage divorcing parents to remain in close contact with their children and to cooperate with each other in matters relating to the children's welfare. It will be a rare situation, however, where the former spouses wish both to share fully in providing physical care for the child and in making decisions on all important matters concerning the child. In fact, full joint custody in this sense is rarely sought or ordered in divorce cases. What joint custody has come to mean in practice is, for the most part, shared *legal* custody, with *physical* custody remaining in one parent, usually the mother. There is very little difference in day-to-day life between this kind of joint custody and the custody arrangement which has been standard for many years, under which the mother has sole legal and physical custody and the father has "reasonable" visitation privileges, except that under joint legal custody the primary caretaker has to share decision-making power.

The virtue of the concept of joint custody is that it may help to focus the attention of parents on the interests of their children after divorce, especially in cases where the relationship between divorcing parents has not severely deteriorated. But relationships between divorcing couples are apt to be at their worst in the months immediately preceding and following the divorce itself. Thus the defect of a statutory preference for joint custody is that, like the best-interests standard, it can be used to force the parent who most wants custody into financial concessions. Joint legal custody involves no major responsibilities for the parent who is not the physical custodian. But it requires the parent who is providing day-to-day care for the child to seek the other parent's consent on important decisions involving the child. Thus mothers, who are still the primary physical custodians in the overwhelming majority of cases, may well reduce their claims for child support in order to avoid having joint legal custody imposed on them. Furthermore, in a contested case, a judge is apt to be tempted to award joint custody, even when the parties are not good candidates for it, simply to avoid having to choose between the parents.

One alternative rule, beginning to attract support, is that adopted in West Virginia in 1981. That state's highest court imposed a limitation on the trial judge's discretion in applying the "best interests of the child" test by adopting a "primary caretaker rule."[102] This rule establishes a strong preference in custody matters for the parent who has provided most of the day-to-day attention to the physical needs of the child: feeding, bathing, driving to school and to see friends, taking responsibility for the child's health needs, and interacting with the child's friends and teachers. The preference is absolute if the primary caretaker is a fit parent and the child is too young to form an opinion about the matter. It is more flexible if the child is older. Obviously, except for its sex-neutrality, this rule looks like the reincarnation of the old and never-quite-dead presumption in favor of maternal custody in cases involving children of tender years. Even after courts and legislatures abandoned the explicit maternal preference, it was still frequently applied in practice. But by making the primary-caretaker presumption explicit and mandatory, West Virginia has gone far toward eliminating the cloud of uncertainty which hung over the divorce negotiating process and permitted many mothers to be frightened into relinquishing needed support. According to Justice Neely, the new rule in West Virginia has "reduced the volume of domestic litigation over children enormously."[103] Apparently, some version of the primary-caretaker preference is already at work modifying the "best interests" standard in the practice of some state courts.[104] Such trends in the case law, accompanied by thoughtful scholarly re-examination of a rule that swept the state legislatures before its implications had been adequately explored, offer the possibility of reintroducing a certain measure of predictability into custody law.

In summary, I have proposed a basic restructuring of divorce law to take account of different categories of divorces. For the largest single category, couples with minor children, I have suggested that first priority in settling the economic effects of such divorces be given to assuring the welfare of the children, with the present (or an improved) system of spousal support and property division brought into play only after this aim has been accomplished. For this new system to work well, it would be desirable to change our tax laws so that tax advantages could be gained for the person who makes periodic payments for a child or children. In the process of determining the amounts of child support, attention must be paid to the actual cost of raising children and to a fair sharing of that cost between the parents. Since the economic and child-related effects of the great majority of divorces are regulated by private agreement, the law must be crafted with a view toward facilitating fair agreements. This means that custody law must be modified to remove pressures on primary caretakers to give up needed financial resources because they fear losing their children; likewise, parents' agreements in cases involving minor children should be carefully reviewed by courts under clear child support standards. A great deal of judicial discretion would remain in a system reformed along these lines. But it would be discretion guided by principles and, if properly supervised by appellate courts, it could be expected to produce in time a body of reasonably coherent case law. This, in turn, would reinforce the basic system for regulating the economic and child-related aspects of divorce, namely private agreement.

Another large group of divorces should be marked off for special treatment. These are the divorces terminating short, childless marriages. Already a few states have recognized that this is a special category that calls for simplified regulation and have established expeditious summary proceedings for divorces that involve no children and in which the spouses have come to a property agreement.[105] There is no reason why the law could not be even more helpful in such cases. What the spouses in these cases need above all is a clear background for negotiation.

At present, in the great majority of states, negotiation in this type of case takes place against the background of discretionary property distribution and alimony statutes. Cases of this sort present the ideal situation for a fixed rule on marital property, such as the old separate property system of "his" and "hers" or the California or Louisiana-style equal division of acquests. These divorces, unlike ones involving couples with minor children, usually can be wound up with a quick, clean break. Possibly, the fixed rules could be softened at the margins by discretion to vary an award in exceptional situations to avoid gross economic unfairness.[106] Introducing discretion in this way would be preferable to the form of discretionary distribution that merely establishes a presumption of equal division. But either a sorting-out of his and hers, or flat invariable equal division, or an equal-division rule with limited discretion to vary, or even discretionary distribution with a presumption in favor of equal division as its starting point is to be preferred over uncontrolled discretion. The last thing in the world these couples need is a statute that says judges can rummage around in all their property and reallocate it in any way that seems fair. So far as spousal support is concerned, in short childless marriages it is usually not sought or awarded, but it would be desirable to make clear that in such cases there is to be no alimony in principle and that short-term rehabilitative awards can be made only in exceptional cases.

While the two categories of divorce I have recommended for special treatment here together represent a substantial majority of all divorces, a number of situations have fallen outside the discussion. Notable among these are divorces in families with grown children, and divorces terminating long childless marriages which may or may not have involved significant economic dependency. The principles that should govern in such cases will be much harder to devise and more apt to be controversial than those in the two groups of cases I have discussed. But it is clear that for these divorces too the present unpredictable American system of divorce law does not work as well as it might, and should be recast to provide a better framework for negotiation.

FROM NO-FAULT TO NO-RESPONSIBILITY DIVORCE?

The recent history of divorce law resembles that of abortion law in that major legal changes have taken place in most Western countries over such a short period of time as to appear almost simultaneous. Countries that differ from each other culturally and politically and are at quite disparate levels of economic development have moved, as if in concert, toward making marriage more freely terminable. Yet a closer examination here, as in the area of abortion, shows the United States taking a somewhat particular and extreme position. When the grounds of divorce are compared, one finds that only Sweden resembles the United States in the degree to which its legal system has accepted unilateral no-fault divorce. When a comparison is made of the legal treatment of the economic consequences of divorce, however, it is apparent that in most places, including Sweden, freer terminability of marriage by no means connotes freedom from economic responsibilities toward former dependents. In fact, the United States appears unique among Western countries in its relative carelessness about assuring either public or private responsibility for the economic casualties of divorce. More than any other country among those examined here, the United States has accepted the idea of no-fault, no-responsibility divorce.

Yet, I hasten to add, this state of affairs seems to have come about more by accident than design. In the first place, the fact that divorce is governed by state law in the United States has played a crucial role. In the family law area, the American federal system has not operated as a laboratory in which various legal approaches could be tested in different states. On the contrary, the opportunity for evasion of one state's marriage or divorce law by migration to another state has made it difficult for any one state to resist for long pressure for conformity to patterns of diminished regulation, once other states begin to move in that direction.

The English and West European divorce laws of recent years emerged from a law reform process that differs from the American in several important respects. Divorce legislation in these countries has nationwide application, so reform proposals are intensely discussed in the national press and on radio and television. The debate achieves a degree of sustained public attention that is never secured by a proposed change in the divorce law of a single American state. Furthermore, any important change in family law in a European country is typically preceded by extensive studies of behavior and opinion in the areas involved. Draft laws are typically accompanied by carefully researched reports or working papers discussing the operation of the existing laws, as well as the likely advantages and disadvantages of proposed changes. On the Continent this work is usually carried out under the direction of full-time staff members of the ministries of justice.[107] In England it falls under the responsibility of the Law Commission, which was created by Parliament in 1965 with a mandate to "take and keep under review all of the law with a view toward systematic development and reform, including in particular codification, elimination of anomalies, repeal of obsolete laws, consolidation, simplification, and modernization of the law."[108] In the United States the practicing matrimonial bar has had much more influence on divorce law reform than it has had or sought in Western Europe.[109] Often this influence has been direct and decisive, as when state legislatures have relied on the presumed expertise of family law sections of local bar associations to draft new legislation. Almost inevitably, divorce lawyers have brought to those tasks a lively concern for their own economic interests. This contrasts markedly with, say, France, where the task of drafting the 1975 divorce law was entrusted to an "elder statesman" of civil law scholars, widely admired for his literary gifts, his gentle wisdom, and his vast knowledge of law and social theory.

Though American divorce law was never intended in principle to be as unusual as it has turned out in fact, it nevertheless carries a powerful ideology, sending out distinctive messages about commitment, responsibility, and dependency. We have examined these messages here, in the law relating to the termination of marriage as such and in the rules concerning the economic consequences of marriage dissolution. The law governing the effects of divorce has the most obvious and immediate impact on people's lives, but it is the ritual termination of marriage that is more highly charged with symbolism. The law concerning the causes for divorce establishes the script for this status-changing rite. Thus changes in the grounds for divorce have often been more controversial than important changes in the rules governing property division and support.

It was for this reason that, in most countries, nonfault divorce along American-Swedish lines was simply not a politically viable option. As we have seen, the preferred compromise of the 1960s and 1970s consisted in the adoption of statutes under which a formal divorce ceremony continued to be available, but which also permitted both spouses to agree openly to divorce, and either spouse to terminate a dead marriage without proof of fault after a period of several years' separation. The various versions of this compromise all had this in common: they officially maintained the idea of marriage as an enduring relationship involving reciprocal rights and obligations. In the absence of mutual consent, this relationship could be terminated only when one spouse seriously breached his or her marital duties, or when the marriage had ceased to function over a long period of time. The extent to which this official story was meant to be serious is indicated by the length of the mandatory separation period for unilateral divorce and the presence or absence of a hardship clause. Whether it is serious in practice depends on how thoroughly the courts actually look into the facts and enforce the law.

Similarly, the story told in the pure nonfault divorce laws—that marriage can be terminated when it ceases to fulfill the expectations of an individual spouse and that divorce is a normal process of transition and adjustment—does not always correspond in practice to reality. In many apparently lenient jurisdictions one spouse can delay the divorce process for a long period of time with disputes over finances or child custody.

What difference, then, do the grounds for divorce make, apart from the role they may play as levers in the bargaining process? Max Rheinstein, in a study published in 1972, found no apparent correlation between the strictness or leniency of divorce law and the incidence of marriage breakdown in various countries.[110] A French comparative study published in 1983 concluded similarly that there was no clear and consistent relationship between changes in the divorce laws and fluctuations in rates of divorce.[111] The reason such studies do not completely put to rest speculation about the consequences of alterations in divorce law, however, is that the effects of changes in legal symbolism are indirect, slow to appear, and hard to disentangle from other social factors. Statute books and case reports are remote from most people's lives, but the imaginative portrayal of family life and ethics in divorce law reaches deeply into our culture—as the law is transmitted in lawyers' offices; in courtrooms; in television news, documentaries, and dramas; in newspapers and popular magazines, and in the cinema. This process of transmission is often a process of transformation, with many slips of meaning along the way. In the United States the "no-fault" idea blended readily with the psychological jargon that already has such a strong influence on how Americans think about their personal relationships.[112] It began to carry the suggestion that no one is ever to blame when a marriage ends:

marriages just break down sometimes, people grow apart, and when this happens even parents have a right to pursue their own happiness. The no-fault terminology fit neatly into an increasingly popular mode of discourse in which values are treated as a matter of taste, feelings of guilt are regarded as unhealthy, and an individual's primary responsibility is assumed to be to himself. Above all, one is not supposed to be "judgmental" about the behavior and opinions of others. As Bellah points out, the ideology of psychotherapy not only refuses to take a moral stand, it actively promotes distrust of "morality."[113]

The American story about marriage, as told in the law and in much popular literature, goes something like this: marriage is a relationship that exists primarily for the fulfillment of the individual spouses. If it ceases to perform this function, no one is to blame and either spouse may terminate it at will. After divorce, each spouse is expected to be self-sufficient. If this is not possible with the aid of property division, some rehabilitative maintenance may be in order for a temporary period. Children hardly appear in the story; at most they are rather shadowy characters in the background. Other stories, of course, are still vigorous in American culture—about marriage as a union for life, for better or worse, even in sickness or poverty; stories about taking on responsibilities and carrying through; and about parenthood as an awesome commitment. But, by and large, they are not the ones that have been incorporated into the law. In the continuing cultural conversation about marriage and family life, American law has weighed in heavily on the side of individual self-fulfillment. It tells us that if a marriage no longer suits our needs or if the continuation of a pregnancy would not fit in with our plans just now, we can choose to sever the relationship.

In most European countries the law has assumed a somewhat different role, incorporating more elements of the ongoing social debate. Where long waiting periods are required for unilateral nonfault divorce, marriage cannot be said to be freely terminable in principle. In many jurisdictions the idea that spouses have definite responsibilities to each other, the violation of which constitutes "fault," still plays an important role, both with respect to the grounds and the economic consequences of divorce.[114] In numerous ways, both practical and symbolic, most legal systems still try to reinforce the idea of marriage as a serious and durable commitment, even in their liberalized divorce law. The 1976 West German divorce law, for example, added to the Civil Code section on the effects of marriage the following sentence: "Marriage is concluded for a lifetime."[115] From one point of view this insertion, part of a last-minute compromise between the coalition government and the Christian Democrats, is strikingly out of place in a divorce statute, just another sop to the losers. Yet, like the opening statement of the 1975 French abortion statute, it acknowledges an important ideal of a large segment of the population, while accommodating to some extent in practice those who do not share or cannot live up to the ideal. It lets us know, too, why the winners did not obtain everything they sought.

In the end one can only speculate about the possible effects of the ideological aspects of divorce law on the way people think and feel about marriage. But one can be somewhat more definite about the effects of different kinds of laws regulating the economic consequences of divorce. We have seen that the most striking contrasts in divorce law among various jurisdictions involve the treatment of children and of those parents who become economically dependent to some degree by virtue of devoting themselves to child care. What are we to make of the fact that the United States has been less ready than most other countries to resort either to force or persuasion in compelling absent parents to pay child support?

The situation in the United States was such in 1982 that a leading academic expert on child support law, David Chambers, could write that he foresaw the day when the United States might greatly curtail compulsory child support, perhaps limiting it to payments over a few years' transitional period as is now often done with alimony, or even eliminate it altogether.[116] He thought some such curtailment was likely because of "changes in the perception of the degree of moral responsibility absent parents bear for their children's support."[117] The "principal messenger" of such changes in attitudes, he said, was the behavior of absent parents themselves.[118] He reviewed the well-known facts that most unmarried parents who have never lived with their children do not pay support at all, while even divorced parents typically make regular payments only for a short time, then decrease them, and then often cease paying altogether. He identified as an "even more global force" for change the fact that women alone with children today can survive at a higher standard of living than in the past "without starving."[119] While careful to say that he did not foresee complete elimination of the father's legal child support obligation so long as women cannot decently maintain families through their own efforts, and government does not step in to fill the breach adequately, Chambers nevertheless maintained that if these things change, "we should be reluctant to retain a system of government-enforced nostalgia for a world that has been lost."[120]

Chambers predicted that not only the United States but "other Western nations" might well abandon the idea of enforcing child support from absent parents.[121] It is interesting to speculate about how most West Europeans would receive this news. On Chambers' reasoning, presumably the countries which provide the most public support to families would be the most likely to move in this direction. But in fact the opposite seems true. Where the most generous public assistance to one-parent families exists, it does not coincide with lax or indifferent attitudes toward enforcing private child support. These days, concern about government spending is as intense in advanced welfare states as it is anywhere else. Sweden, the country with the largest package of benefits and services for children, places first-line responsibility for child support squarely upon the parents, and enforces it rigorously. Public responsibility thus seems to reinforce private. The various American states, on the other hand, most of which provide public benefits at a relatively low level, have been a good deal less insistent on seeing that child support is assessed at a reasonable level and that it is paid.

The most serious flaw in Chambers' reasoning, however, is his linking the fact that many absent parents have decreased the amount or ceased to make their support payments with the conclusion that ideas about the morality of paying child support have changed. As the West European experience indicates, and as Chambers' own studies in Michigan show, law and law enforcement have a great deal to do with behavior in this area.[122] The existence of efficient and vigorous enforcement measures produces a high rate of compliance in certain Michigan counties and in Sweden. As for the alleged diminishing sense of moral responsibility, whose sense are we talking about? Do mothers who receive no child support feel that it is not the moral responsibility of the child's father to share the economic burdens of raising the child? Do taxpayers feel it is primarily their responsibility to care for the children of broken families? If the diminished sense of moral responsibility Chambers is talking about is just that of defaulting fathers, is it merely "nostalgia" to maintain a different notion of morality in the law?

What Chambers dismisses as nostalgia is precisely what Geertz tells us is an important function of law—that of interpreting our culture to ourselves, of summing up our ideals while at the same time reinforcing them. If law has an interpretive and constitutive function, then changing the law so as to eliminate a duty where one has long existed cannot help but have some effect on behavior and attitudes. Once again, with divorce law as with abortion law, we find in the United States a very uncritical attitude toward conforming law to widespread patterns of behavior, with little attention given to the role that law itself may play in forming attitudes and channeling behavior. American divorce law in practice seems to be saying to parents, especially mothers, that it is not safe to devote oneself primarily or exclusively to raising children.

THREE

WHY THE AMERICAN DIFFERENCE?

Starting in the late 1960s, both abortion law and divorce law underwent profound and rapid change in Western countries. Viewed from afar, the direction of change was broadly similar everywhere: divorce and legal abortions became more readily available. The substantive differences between American law and the laws of other countries on abortion and divorce were, for the most part, differences of degree. Nevertheless, it is striking that major changes in both divorce and abortion law during this period took place first in the United States and England, and that the changes took an extreme form in American law. Today, abortion is subject to less regulation in the United States than in any other country in the Western world. So far as divorce is concerned, the United States is not unique in having made marriage terminable virtually at the will of either party. But the country as a whole is set apart by its relative lack of concern with assuring either public or, until very recently, private responsibility for the problems of dependency associated with changing patterns of family behavior.

Besides the differences in the content of laws and programs related to abortion, divorce, and economic dependency, I have called attention to more subtle divergences having to do with form, style, and tone. Constitutions, statutes, and court decisions in the continental countries are more deeply engaged in an ongoing moral conversation about abortion, divorce, and dependency than are their Anglo-American counterparts. The Scandinavian countries are something of a special case. Though casting their laws in a neutral, bureaucratic form, they communicate strong messages about parental responsibility for children and society's responsibility for the well-being of each of its members.

If we turn from how family law and policy look now to where they may be heading, it is fair to say that in all the countries discussed here, with the possible exception of Ireland, they seem to be drifting in roughly the same general direction. There is little observable inclination to impose more restrictions on abortion and none at all for making it more difficult to dissolve the bonds of matrimony, although many countries have made divorce more costly by tightening up their laws regarding financial responsibilities of family members to each other. But at the same time, in spite of long-standing European policies and programs to aid families with children, such families (especially if they are headed by women) seem to be in a more or less precarious position everywhere.

Despite the convergence, the differences of degree remain significant, and the puzzles we began with persist: Why did American law, more than others, come to embody the idea that termination of a marriage or a pregnancy was a matter of individual right? Why has the United States shown less readiness than most countries at comparable levels of development to deal with those forms of economic dependency that especially affect women and children?

One thing seems clear. No one set out deliberately to tell the kind of story that is currently being told in American abortion and divorce law. The tale told by the law in these areas is reminiscent of Robert Bellah's observation that contemporary Americans have difficulty articulating the richness of their personal commitments, and that they "frequently live out a fuller sense of purpose in life than they can justify in rational terms."[1] Bellah and his co-authors sought out Americans in all walks of life and asked them to talk about what was most important to them. They found that the men and women interviewed were unable to express themselves in other than what Bellah called their "first language" of individualism, and he surmised that this language made "their lives sound more isolated and arbitrary than . . . they actually are."[2] In the same way, perhaps, our legal vocabulary and imagination have been inadequate to the task of telling the kind of story most Americans would want to tell about the sad and complex issues involved in divorce and abortion.

But if that is so, the question becomes: where did the legal story come from? Can we, out of the multiplicity of factors that go into the making of a body of law, identify some which were especially influential in the United States and less so elsewhere, or vice versa? In part, many of the American developments appear to be examples of the Athenian Stranger's observation in *The Laws* that chance and accident legislate for us in all sorts of ways.[3] But it also seems that there are certain types of accidents to which we Americans have been particularly susceptible. The story we tell in our family law may not quite be the one we meant to tell, but it is recognizably related to other stories that we like very much, stories we tell ourselves, each other, and our children over and over again—about self-reliance, individual liberty, and tolerance for diversity.

This line of thought gives rise to some further questions. How are self-reliance, individual liberty, and tolerance related to selfish indifference, isolation, and nihilism? At what point does the language of individualism in a society or in a legal system begin crowding out other modes of discourse? When one has lost the ability to speak or even to form concepts in other ways, can one really be said to be living a richer and fuller life than one can express? Does a country or legal system which gives highest priority to individualistic values come to be inhabited only by persons who put those values above all others and act accordingly? Is the legal system promoting as well as reflecting such a tendency?

A WORD TOCQUEVILLE'S ANCESTORS DID NOT KNOW

A full account of how a certain way of thinking and speaking achieved priority in our legal system would have to begin with a cultural explanation, too long and complicated to undertake here. Various thinkers have called attention to the ways in which English society seems to have facilitated, at an early stage, the rise of the free, self-determining individual.[4] I will only allude briefly here to some of the features of the Anglo-American societies that made them fertile ground for this development.

Tocqueville, in his essay on the French revolution, wrote of the word "individualism" that it "was unknown to our ancestors, for the good reason that in their days every individual necessarily belonged to a group and no one could regard himself as an isolated unit."[5] By "individualism" Tocqueville did not mean either egoism or the desire to fulfill the highest potential of the self, but rather the tendency to conceive of the self apart from social context and interpersonal relationships. But though it may be true that the word was yet to be found, the process through which the old feudal society of groups was giving way to the new society of individuals and the modern centralized state was already well under way in Europe even at the time of the *ancien régime*. Individualism in the sense that Tocqueville used the word was not only emerging as a social phenomenon, but it had decisively entered the world of ideas through the Renaissance, the Cartesian theory of knowledge, and the emphasis of the reformed religions on the relationship of man and God without intermediaries. Nevertheless, it was the French Revolution which turned the phenomenon into a political program. The revolutionary slogan, "There are no rights except those of individuals and the State," was the political analog of Reformation theology. It was directed against all the *corps intermédiaires* of the old regime.[6] In particular, churches, craft associations, and the family were seen as oppressive to the individual and as a threat to consolidation of the nation-state.

The revolutionary government vigorously pursued its political program through legislation abolishing guilds, instituting unilateral divorce, and confiscating the property of the Church. But this aspect of the French Revolution did not long survive. Napoleon quickly re-established a special position for the Catholic Church which lasted until 1905, and he promoted the development of other churches with public funds.[7] In the Civil Code of 1804, following Roman law tradition, the law stopped at the threshhold of the home, and within the home the husband and father reigned supreme.[8] Divorce was completely abolished in 1816, shortly after the restoration of the Bourbon monarchy, and was not permitted again in France until 1884. The old society of groups continued to disintegrate, of course, but it did so slowly. Old patterns, ties, and attitudes had been too deeply rooted in France, and on the European continent generally, to be displaced overnight, even by the mighty forces unleashed by the French Revolution.

Modern ideas about individual liberty found more hospitable soil, however, in a country where the breakup of what we now call feudalism had begun earlier than on the Continent. Free markets in land, the loosening of the connection between family and land, and social mobility based on wealth all emerged earlier in England than elsewhere.[9] Not only did our English ancestors emerge from a different form of feudalism than Tocqueville's did, they embarked earlier on the transition from a highly organized institutional religion, whose individual members are conceived of as forming one mystical body, to various religions which stress the individual and downplay the role of mediating structures. Furthermore, t] were more affected by the culture of the Enlightenment. No nation's boundaries could hold back the pervasive influence of the ideas of that period about man, nature, reason, science, and political society. But some countries were more deeply penetrated than others. Though it was French philosophers who immodestly gave themselves the name *Lumières,* French society in general was not so congenial to the new culture as were England, Holland, Denmark, Prussia, and Scotland. In France, as in southern Europe, Ireland, and Russia, the gap between the ideas of the educated minority and the social and political life of the country as a whole was considerably greater than in several of its Northern European neighbors.[10]

As for the English colonies that became the United States, where a certain restlessness and rootlessness were built in from the beginning, there were even fewer obstacles to the spread either of the idea or the practice of individualism.[11] Cultural diversity was there from the first, too, for the English were not the only colonists or immigrants on the new continent. Though the early settlers had nurtured an ideal of community, much of American history in the first two centuries after settlement involves the development of a refusal to live by any such idea.[12] By the mid-nineteenth century the United States was already one of the most fluid and unstructured societies the civilized world had ever seen.[13] Despite pockets of resistance, the ideal of the free, self-reliant, self-determining individual had won the day. To a foreign observer like Tocqueville, it was the pervasiveness of the phenomenon that seemed amazing:

> An American will build a house in which to pass his old age and sell it before the roof is on; he will plant a garden and rent it just as the trees are coming into bearing; he will clear a field and leave others to reap the harvest; he will take up a profession and leave it, settle in one place and soon go off elsewhere with his changing desires . . .
>
> Death steps in in the end and stops him before he has grown tired of this futile pursuit of that complete felicity which always escapes him.
>
> At first sight there is something astonishing in this spectacle of so many lucky men restless in the midst of abundance. But it is a spectacle as old as the world; all that is new is to see a whole people performing in it.[14]

In a country where, as Tocqueville observed, "neither law nor custom holds anyone in one place,"[15] the powerful rhetoric of liberty was bound to strike a different chord than it did among people who lived their entire lives within a relatively short radius from their birthplace.

Tocqueville himself underestimated the Americans' power to resist the community-destroying forces that were already at work in nineteenth-century American society. His main preoccupation, quite naturally, was the centralization of political authority in France, which he feared would cause the democratic experiment there to end in tyranny. He thought he saw social factors in the United States that could counter such a trend. For one thing, Americans seemed to him to be a nation of joiners, busily forming all kinds of associations.[16] More important, he considered that, in the then decentralized United States, small communities like the New England townships would serve as schools for citizenship where the maximum possible number of people could develop a clear, practical conception not only of their rights, but of their duties.[17] Americans governing their towns would learn a taste for order and formality, without which, he said, "freedom can advance only through revolutions."[18]

Within the American family, he believed, women (as the main

teachers of children and keepers of orderly, peaceful homes) would play a key role in transmitting the republican virtues of self-restraint and concern for the common good.[19] Like many high-minded American intellectuals of the day—indeed like the Founders themselves—Tocqueville expected that families and churches would moderate the effects of individual greed, selfishness, and ambition. The Founders seem to have taken for granted that the individual would be situated within the family, and the family within a small community, nested like Chinese boxes. But that state of affairs began to be eroded earlier than is generally supposed. The effects of that erosion were clearly visible by the early years of the present century, even though many contemporary Americans tend to see that time as one when family values were strong and American families were stable. It is sobering to realize that American divorce rates in the "good old days," while low compared to what we are experiencing now, were at least double, and often triple or quadruple those of any European country.[20]

Small, vigorous communities necessarily compete for power with the state; they also constrain individual freedom. They lost out on both counts: in the process of centralization of public power, as well as with the rise of the free, self-determining individual. When the Founders debated and worried about what they called factions, it was no doubt difficult even to imagine a world in which small towns would become suburbs, urban neighborhoods would be uprooted, religion would be banished from the public square, craft associations would be confined to a narrowly economic role, and individual choice would render family ties increasingly fluid, detachable, and interchangeable. Flourishing associations and communities of various sorts were once not only islands of countervailing power, but also places where the skills of governing and a certain independence of mind could be developed. They are therefore to be distinguished from contemporary single-issue interest groups, or the group-egoism of what Bellah calls "lifestyle enclaves."[21] As communities of memory, solidarity, hope, and long-term commitment become weak, societies begin to experience the reverse of the condition that prevailed under the various forms of feudalism on the Continent: while social historians have had to look hard to find little islands of individualism there in the

Middle Ages,[22] social scientists have to strain to discover latent networks of community and kinship in contemporary America.

Americans are of course justly proud of their tradition of political freedom and of the high value they place on the individual person. We are rightly accustomed to viewing our self-reliance and independence as sources of some of our greatest strengths. And we are in general highly sensitive to the disastrous consequences that underemphasis on these values has had in certain twentieth-century regimes. We are less conscious, however, of the dangers that Tocqueville warned us could flow from overemphasizing them. As he pointed out, the isolated modern individual is especially vulnerable to and manipulable by despotism:

> What can even public opinion do when not even a *score* of people are held together by any common bond, when there is no man, no family, no body, no class, and no free association which can represent public opinion and set it in motion?
>
> When each citizen being equally impotent, poor, and isolated cannot oppose his individual weakness to the organized force of the government?[23]

As for "public opinion," Tocqueville elsewhere called attention to its profound ambiguity: the isolated individual in a regime of equality is not only susceptible to political domination, but also to a kind of soft tyranny in which one's ability to think for oneself is lost. Thus, in the end, a people in a country where liberty has been severed from other republican virtues can paradoxically display both individualism and conformity, restlessness and huddling, rejection of authority and political impotence.

THE LONG SHADOW OF HOBBES

Partly because of its somewhat different experience with, and earlier emergence from, feudalism, England seems to have been especially receptive to modern notions of rights and individualism, which encountered more social resistance in the continental countries. This was even more the case in the restless and heterogeneous society of the United States. But this is not the place to recapitulate what historians and social scientists have said about

English and American ideas about individual liberty. What I wish to explore here is a less well examined aspect of the phenomenon: the way in which Anglo-American *law* was susceptible to assimilating modern notions of individual liberty in a more unrestricted form than the civil law systems were. This legal difference seems attributable not only to social factors, but also in part to happenings in the world of ideas: first, by the fact that the common law and civil law systems were influenced, in form and content, by different types of linkage with political theory; and second, by the effect that different branches of Enlightenment thought had on Anglo-American and continental legal mentalities, respectively. I will argue that Anglo-American legal attitudes toward abortion, divorce, and dependency bear the unmistakable traces of certain modern ideas about law that were not so fully accepted on the Continent. Then I will try to demonstrate how the continental legal treatment of these subjects was affected by the survival of some older ideas about law that were more thoroughly rooted out of the common law systems.

A discussion of the new ideas that had such an influence on Anglo-American law must begin with Thomas Hobbes, because the common law tradition, to a greater extent than we may care to recognize, absorbed the Hobbesian myth of man in the state of nature as an isolated, self-interested creature of fear and desire, engaged in a perpetual state of war with everyone else, and driven into political society only for the sake of self-preservation. This myth, as everyone knows, entails a certain anthropology and a radical new political theory. But what is less well known is that it also entails a certain legal philosophy. Hobbes was consciously breaking with the venerable English legal tradition, as well as with the traditional Christian view of man and society, and with classical political philosophy. Among other things, he set out deliberately to demolish the idea of law that he associated with Lord Coke: the idea of law as the "perfection of reason"—a kind of collective wisdom "fined and refined" over centuries by long experience and by the contributions of "an infinite number of grave and learned men."[24] In place of Coke's memorable formulation, Hobbes put forward what is now a widely accepted modern definition of law as the command of the sovereign, resting not on long use and acceptance, but on power.[25] For Coke's corporate reason, Hobbes substituted calculating reason and *raison d'état*.

I have described these ideas as modern. But of course they were well known in classical political philosophy as foils to be discredited in argument. What is modern is only that, with Machiavelli, they began to be put forward seriously, and, with Hobbes and others, they began to become respectable. But they did not achieve acceptance overnight. The common law of Hobbes's day was sublimely indifferent to his legal ideas and remained so until long after his death when they had become dissociated from his name. As late as the mid-eighteenth century, with parliamentary legislation only sporadic, and judicial decisions the main source of law, Blackstone could still convincingly affirm that the common law of England was the custom of the realm from time immemorial.[26] Blackstone's *Commentaries,* for all their preliminary nodding in the direction of Locke, and their formal acknowledgment of absolute parliamentary sovereignty, are a treatise of, by, and for the common-law lawyer.

What, then, brought the Leviathan up from the deep and into the mainstream of Anglo-American law? The sharp distinction Hobbes had drawn between law and morality, and his idea of law as command backed up by the threat of force, were brought to the forefront of English legal theory only in the nineteenth century by Jeremy Bentham and John Austin who, unlike Hobbes, did not call themselves moral philosophers. But it was that redoubtable and long-lived American, O. W. Holmes, Jr., who was particularly instrumental in the process through which these ideas became not only intellectually respectable but dominant in one of the world's major legal systems.

Meanwhile, in England, a powerful set of formulations about individual liberty had been worked out by a young disciple of Bentham and Austin whose influence among his contemporaries far exceeded theirs. The case of John Stuart Mill is particularly interesting because it illustrates how the law simplifies and reshapes ideas in the process of incorporating them into its own framework, and because the direct influence of Mill's political ideas upon law in England and the United States has been documented in so many ways. Mill's prestige in his day, especially among the young, was enormous. As Dicey recounts in his lectures on law and public opinion in England, the essay *On Liberty* "appeared to thousands of admiring disciples to provide the final and conclusive demonstration of the absolute truth of individualism, and to establish on firm ground the doctrine that the protection of freedom was the one great object of wise law and sound policy."[27]

In the essay *On Liberty* Mill set forth the now-familiar principle: "The only purpose for which power can be rightfully exercised over any member of a civilised community, against his will, is to prevent harm to others."[28] The underlying idea of the essay is less familiar. It was Mill's dream that classical and modern political theory could be reconciled—that democracy could be ennobled (and tyranny of the majority prevented) by making it possible for all individuals, not just gentlemen, to become wise and virtuous. But as Mill's thoughts on liberty found their way into legal, and eventually popular discourse, they did so in a somewhat distorted form. The essay lent itself to being restated later as more of a manifesto of moral relativism than it really was. The John Stuart Mill who had distinguished between higher and lower pleasures was ignored, and his defense of freedom of speech and conduct was detached from his aim of democratizing the classical virtues. His thought blended all too easily with ideas he did not himself accept of the relativity and equal worth of all opinions and life styles.

It is now quite forgotten, for example, that Mill himself took a stern position with respect to the responsibilities of parents toward children. In fact, his stated justification for having a general theory of liberty was that, without a general principle, liberty not only is often withheld where it should be granted, but is just as often granted where it should be withheld.[29] His prime examples of improper *grants* of liberty were drawn from family relations: "[M]isplaced notions of liberty prevent moral obligations on the part of parents from being recognised, and legal obligations from being imposed, where there are the strongest grounds for the former always, and in many cases for the latter also."[30] He was highly critical of the traditional English policy of nonintervention in the ongoing family.

It still remains unrecognised, that to bring a child into existence without a fair prospect of being able, not only to provide food for its body, but instruction and training for its mind, is a moral crime, both against the unfortunate offspring and against society; and that if the parent does not fulfil this obligation, the State ought to see it fulfilled, at the charge, as far as possible, of the parent.[31]

Contrary to the spirit of the recent United States Supreme Court decision in *Zablocki v. Redhail*,[32] the great modern apostle of liberty thought that even the right to marry properly could be subordinated to the obligation to pay child support.

The laws which, in many countries on the Continent, forbid marriage unless the parties can show that they have the means of supporting a family, do not exceed the legitimate powers of the State: and whether such laws be expedient or not (a question mainly dependent on local circumstances and feelings), they are not objectionable as violations of liberty.[33]

In matters touching the family (and here Mill may have had in mind not only parents' obligations to their children, but the complete freedom to disinherit spouse and children that then existed in England), he said that English notions of liberty could easily lead one to suppose that "a man had an indispensable right to do harm to others, and no right at all to please himself without giving pain to anyone."[34] As for divorce, although Mill held that, in principle, one ought to be free to dissolve a marriage at will, he conceded that reliance by one party might change this, and that the interests of children must at least be a factor, if not a bar.[35]

Though this side of Mill has been for the most part forgotten, there has been no misunderstanding of the fact that the essay *On Liberty* was meant to and did represent a great expansion of the notion of rights in the Anglo-American world, which already had a long tradition of discourse about rights. For Hobbes only life itself, and for Locke only life, property, and a limited concept of liberty were rights, secure as such from the state. Then came Mill, claiming that a much larger area of human conduct and opinion should be free from governmental interference. He thus gave the long-standing English tradition of noninterference with private life a theoretical justification. Introduced through Justices Holmes, Brandeis, and others, many of Mill's ideas grounded crucial steps in American law and entered popular culture, giving us the "marketplace of ideas," the "clear and present danger" test, the notion of the consenting adult, and the right to be let alone, which Warren and Brandeis recast in their famous 1890 law review article as a right of privacy.

What entered Anglo-American law was not the thought of Mill in all its earnestness and inconsistency, or even the whole of his message on liberty, but a version of his views with his moral seriousness and hierarchy of goods sheared off. Thus streamlined, the new version of individual liberty was ready to be reinforced in the twentieth century by the pervasive jargon and world view of psychotherapy. The distinction between respect for the opinions of others and the notion that all ideas are equally worthwhile has been obscured. It did not help that O. W. Holmes, much more of a descendant of Hobbes than Mill was, played such a crucial role as theorist, judge, and phrase-maker in the formative stages of modern American law. (Miss Fannie Dixwell of Boston, searching for the perfect wedding gift for Holmes, showed that she knew her man well by selecting a 1651 first edition of the *Leviathan*.)[36]

In the United States we had little in our tradition to help us resist the advance of ideas of law simply as command, and justice as either a matter of individual opinion or as whatever the law says it is. So long as court decisions were our principal source of law, case law was the vehicle par excellence for maintaining continuity with the past, incorporating new ideas, and adapting the law to changed circumstances.[37] Though less visible than the continental codes, our judicial opinions were often deeply engaged in teaching, story-telling, and elaborating substantive ideas of justice. In its glory, the common law was practical reason in action, and there are still areas where it can operate this way.[38] But increasingly, case law has been displaced by statutory and administrative regulation and has lost much of its strength and coherence.[39]

Although they were by no means immune to positivism and relativism, the continental countries, and even England, had more of an inheritance of other views, which remained more vigorous countercurrents within their traditions. Countervailing tendencies have of course always been present in the United States, too, but they are weaker, perhaps because of our greater cultural diversity. Doubtless one reason we Americans were quicker to translate the new ideology of tolerance into a posture of legal neutrality toward most controversial issues was that this was an especially handy approach to a problem that was more acute in the American system than in others: finding a way to accommodate in the law increasing demands for recognition of our unusual heterogeneity. The continental legal tradition, on the other hand, developed a somewhat different manner of coping with modernity.

THE *LUMIÈRES* AND THEIR
"PASSION FOR LAWS"

Just as continental European society proved somewhat more impervious to the spread of autonomous individualism, the Romano-Germanic legal tradition presented more impediments to the acceptance of certain modern ideas about law. It is true that contemporary civil and common law systems are all operating within a common horizon framed by natural rights theories. But it seems to have made a difference that these theories were elaborated for us by Hobbes and Locke, and for them by Rousseau and Kant. Again, the differences are ones of degree, but they are significant. Although Rousseau, like Hobbes and Locke, accepted the principle of modern natural right, he mounted a devastating critique of Hobbes in the name of classical thought and of a very different idea of nature. Rousseau's attempt to temper Hobbes's notions of freedom and rights with classical ideas of duty and virtue had a lasting impact on continental legal theory.

This is not to say that Rousseau's thought, any more than Mill's, was well understood or accepted in its entirety by the society that paid him homage. A more complex and profound thinker than Mill, Rousseau lent himself even more to being misinterpreted. In the decade before the French Revolution, Rousseau had become the object of an extraordinary cult. Revolutionary orators and pamphleteers capitalized on the popular adulation of the deceased philosopher, ransacking his work for inspiring ideas and stirring phrases.[40] Though Rousseau's influence was thus pervasive, his ideas were mediated through "a panoply of misreadings, mapped according to divergent interests, motivated by a variety of social situations, shaped by the onrush of unforeseen events, [all] facilitated by the ambiguities and tensions contained in Rousseau's own style of writing."[41] In this way, Rousseau helped to keep alive in the civil law certain classical notions which ultimately had little place in his own philosophy.

The course of modernization of French law makes the point, not only with respect to France but concerning the many countries which took French law as a model. In contrast to England, where a unified system of national law began to emerge from the King's Courts at Westminster in the thirteenth century, France until the nineteenth century remained a country where, as Voltaire once put it, a traveler changed his law as often as he changed his horse. The laws of the several regions of France, like those in most of the rest of continental Europe, were composed in varying degrees of an amalgam of customary and Roman law.[42]

The confluence of four factors was of the utmost importance for the form French law took when national legal unification finally occurred. First, there had been a great revival of interest among eighteenth-century French philosophers in customary law and in what the ancients had said about law. This would have been of little importance were it not for the second factor—that French revolutionaries and the statesmen of the Napleonic era were open to the ideas of philosophers in a way that even Plato would have been hard put to imagine. Third, the period after the French Revolution was one of intense legislative activity. And finally, law making in this crucial formative period mainly took the form of legislation. With the French Revolution, as Jean Carbonnier has put it, "a passion for laws," or "a sort of legislative fever seized the body politic."[43] This remarkable enthusiasm for legislation manifested itself in countless ways, from the founding of a club in Paris in 1790 called the Nomophiles, to a literary fascination with the mythical lawgivers of ancient Sparta.[44]

Although law was central, too, to the thought of the founders of the American republic, they were accustomed to viewing law in a different way. To these statesmen "law" meant primarily the common law, the massive accretion of court decisions from ancient

times to the present in which generations of judges—"living oracles" as Blackstone called them—found and declared the principles that had always constituted the custom of the realm.[45] Within
the common law, supplemented from time to time by parliamentary enactments, the "rights of Englishmen" had taken shape,
and by the common law, so the Founders believed, these rights had
been preserved through many a trying time.[46] The American
founders, no less than the French, thus tended to look to law as a
way in which life in society could be brought under the control of
reason. But where the French turned to abstract reason and legislation, the Americans relied more heavily on practical reason, a
constitutional framework, and—despite the fact that they had rejected English rule—the common law tradition. The creative en-
ergy that went into constitution-making in America was devoted
in France to legislation and codification, mainly on private law
subjects. The difference is important, because it meant that in the
late eighteenth and early nineteenth centuries, while American
lawyers and statesmen were giving their best efforts to devising the
structure of government, the French were concentrating theirs
primarily on the legal ordering of the relations of citizens with
each other in the contexts of tort, contract, property, succession,
and family law. In early nineteenth-century America these matters
were largely left to be worked out by judges.

The mania for statutory law in France was accompanied by an
intense preoccupation with education. This was probably not a
coincidence, since these were the twin obsessions of Rousseau,
whose influence on the French founders was, in its way, as great as
that of John Locke on ours. In *The Social Contract, Emile,* and
other works, we find most of the elements that gave French law its
new direction: the near-mystical exaltation of law and the lawgiver, the classical view of the role of law as leading the citizens
toward virtue, and the notion that the effectiveness of law ultimately rests on education and persuasion. Nothing could be more
alien to the spirit in which English common law had evolved,
under the leadership of judges who purported to be finding rather
than making law, than Rousseau's apostrophes to lawmakers. In a
sort of hymn to "The Legislator" which he placed at the very heart
of *The Social Contract,* Rousseau says:

He who dares to undertake the making of a people's institutions ought to feel himself capable, so to speak, of changing human nature, of transforming each individual, who is by himself a complete and solitary whole, into part of a greater whole from which he in a manner receives his life and being; of altering man's constitution for the purpose of strengthening it.[47]

As for the law itself, Rousseau, in his *Discourse on Political Economy,* becomes ecstatic:

How can it be that all should obey, yet nobody take it upon him to command, and that all should serve, and yet have no masters? These wonders are the work of law. It is to law alone that men owe justice and liberty . . . It is this celestial voice which dictates to each citizen the precepts of public reason, and teaches him to act according to the rules of his own judgment, and not to behave inconsistently with himself.[48]

Rousseau, in these passages, was pursuing his attack on Hobbes. Deeming that calculation and self-interest were an insufficient basis for civil society, Rousseau believed that legislation would play a crucial role in teaching people to prefer the common good to their private interest.[49] As a kind of artificial substitute for the compassion that Rousseau believed man possessed in the state of nature, legislation would help to transform self-centered individuals into citizens.

In the United States the notion that law could or should be a transforming force was confined primarily to the constitutional realm, where the lesson of the day was liberty. Most American lawyers of the late eighteenth and early nineteenth century, steeped as they were in Blackstone,[50] would have recoiled from the suggestion that private law had a significant pedagogical role, just as in the mid-nineteenth century they would reject the proposals of Jeremy Bentham and David Dudley Field that the time had come for the common law to be made more rational through systematic codification along continental lines. Legislation then, as now, was thought to be little more than a set of words on paper until it began to acquire meaning in the process of being applied by judges in particular cases. Madison stated the common understanding in Federalist No. 37 when he observed: "All new laws, though penned with the greatest technical skill and passed on the fullest and most mature deliberation, are considered as more or less obscure and equivocal, until their meaning be liquidated and ascertained by a series of particular discussions and adjudications."[51]

French jurists, by contrast, exalted the legislature (which, following Rousseau, they habitually personify even today as "The Legislator"). For most of the nineteenth century French legal writers grossly understated the role of judges in the interpretive process. For their part, postrevolutionary French judges, mindful of the hostility provoked by judicial excesses in the *ancien régime*, kept a low profile, pretending to be "applying" legislative norms even when the law was silent, ambiguous, or incomplete.[52]

Ideas about the hortatory role of law, couched in the rhetoric of civil religion, were very much in the air when the great continental codification movements began. The code draftsmen combined a passion for law with what now seems to us a touching faith in the power of reason to order human affairs. But the French codifiers, unlike the revolutionary legislators, were practical men of affairs and good disciples of Montesquieu. Thus there was room in their legislative scheme for custom and tradition. The legal inheritance of customary and Roman law, "the wisdom of our fathers,"[53] was to be put through the sieve of reason. All that passed through it would be conserved, clarified, and systematized.[54]

The codifications of enlightened monarchs such as Frederick II of Prussia, Joseph II of Austria, and Napoleon were to a great extent conscious attempts to synthesize the political and philosophical thought of the eighteenth century. They were monuments to the idea that a rational, clear, and comprehensive legal system could be constructed on scientific principles. It was taken as obvious that the codifications represented a great improvement over the traditional Romanist and customary law upon which they rested. The French Civil Code of 1804, with its lapidary formulations, its preference for general principles over detailed regulation, and its aim to be accessible to every citizen, was widely regarded as the epitome of enlightened law making. Napoleon, who wanted to be remembered with Solon and Justinian as a great law giver, near the end of his life referred to the code as a more glorious achievement than all his victories: "One Waterloo wipes out their memory, but my Civil Code will last forever."

And indeed, spread not only by conquest and colonization but also by admiring imitation, French law and French ideas about law have had an enormous impact on the civil law around the world, including many parts that later came under the influence of the German Civil Code of 1900 or the principles of Marxism-Leninism. To a greater extent than does Anglo-American law, the civil law systems retain vestiges of the classical view of law as educational. The great codifications, especially those modeled on the French, kept alive a certain rhetorical tradition of statutory drafting and a certain story-telling aspect of law that is notably absent from the Anglo-American legislative tradition. The word "vestiges" is used advisedly. I do not wish to underrate the extent to which continental law, like English and American law, came under the sway of positivism and adopted flat, bureaucratic, neutral, modes of expression. The civil codes, with their majestic style and great principles, are today less central to contemporary civil law systems than the mass of fragmentary statutory and administrative regulations, which have similarly displaced case law as the primary source of law in the Anglo-American systems.

Still, there are occasions on which the old tradition comes to life. In France this happened in connection with abortion and divorce law reform. So far as the 1975 abortion law is concerned, this may have been happenstance. But with regard to divorce law it was very much to be expected, since divorce is regulated in the Civil Code. Amendment of the French Civil Code is a great event—more comparable to constitutional change than to passing a new statute. The public is aware that a national monument of sorts is involved. The importance the French attribute to the task is evidenced by the fact that a very special architect was called in to make the renovations. The task of drafting the divorce reform (along with all other important changes in the family law sections of the French Civil Code in the past twenty years) was entrusted by successive Ministers of Justice to Jean Carbonnier. He was chosen not only because he is a widely respected civil law scholar, but probably also because his literary style is much admired. Where the Civil Code is concerned, form and style are considered to be almost as important as content.

Carbonnier himself, however, is more of a follower of Montesquieu than of Rousseau. The author of several works on legal sociology as well as civil law, he has said that his leading idea in drafting the family law reforms was to accommodate a plurality of views in French society, not to affect ideas and behavior.[55] But in his wording of the 1975 divorce reform he was able to incorporate within the law a conversation that was going on in French society about the circumstances and conditions under which divorce should be made available. He judged that this conversation was based on certain widely shared assumptions, among them that unilateral divorce on demand is unacceptable, and that child-rearing always, and marriage sometimes, involve lasting economic responsibility. His prescriptions were adapted to what a society in the grip of modernity could swallow, but Carbonnier is no slave doctor. As even Rousseau had to acknowledge, "the wise legislator does not begin by laying down laws good in themselves, but by investigating the fitness of the people, for which they are destined, to receive them."[56]

In comparing Anglo-American laws affecting the family with those of the civil law systems, it is important not to exaggerate the contrasts. As I have stressed, both legal traditions have been strongly influenced by the idea of law as command, the rights mode of discourse, and individualism. But on the Continent these ideas were softened, deflected, and counterbalanced to a greater extent by classical and customary notions of law. They took from Montesquieu and his followers an awareness of how culture shapes law, and from Rousseau and his followers a belief that law can help to shape society and the individuals who compose it. Anglo-American, and especially American, law has placed greater emphasis on individual rights, while the civil law systems in varying degrees have moderated this emphasis with more attention to social context and individual responsibility. The difference in emphasis is subtle, but its spirit penetrates every detail of the respective legal systems.

The most ringing endorsement of individual rights in the French legal tradition, the Declaration of the Rights of Man and the Citizen of August 26, 1789, states in its preamble that its purpose is to serve as a constant reminder to the members of the body social, not only of their rights but of their duties.[57] And in the nineteenth-century French and German Civil Codes, though freedom of contract and protection of private property are as centrally important as they were in English and American law, they are qualified in their inception. The French Civil Code of 1804, for example, declares that: "Property is the right to enjoy and dispose of things in the most absolute manner, provided that it is not used in contravention of laws and regulations."[58] Contrast this with the Blackstonian description widely accepted well into the nineteenth century of the right of property as "that sole and despotic dominion which one man claims and exercises over the external things of the world, in total exclusion of the right of any other individual in the universe."[59] As for freedom of contract, the same article of the French Civil Code which establishes it also provides that all contracts must be performed in good faith.[60]

In like manner, a greater tempering of individual rights shows up in many of the details of French and German private law. This was so even at the height of laissez-faire in the late nineteenth and early twentieth century. While Anglo-American common law by the turn of the century had more readily accepted a mythology of self-reliance, the civil law systems were more influenced by the politics of compassion of Rousseau and his followers. In the civil law systems, the concept of abuse of right and the duty of good faith prevented contract, tort, and property law from taking private rights quite to the extremes often found in American law of the period. For example, French and German law quite early worked out limitations on the power of an employer to fire an at-will employee for any or no reason.[61] Under the French and German civil codes, a married property owner was not free to disinherit his children, or even to make large gifts to the detriment of the family.[62] One might mention, too, the legal duty to rescue, so typical in civil law systems, and so indigestible to Anglo-American law.[63]

In the late nineteenth century, when many American courts and treatise writers were preoccupied with the protection of private rights, legislatures in the various American states were extremely active, as were their European counterparts, in passing social legislation. Responding to increasingly broader constituencies (as did the French Third Republic) or to fear of militant socialism (as did

Bismarck's Germany), legislatures in Western countries adopted factory legislation, workmen's compensation laws, rudimentary social welfare laws, and began to regulate commerce and public utilities. Only in the United States, however, was such legislation subject to judicial review—with the well-known consequences that followed when state and federal courts saw many of these laws as interfering with private property and freedom of contract. In other countries the courts could, and to some extent did, limit the effectiveness of such legislation by restrictive interpretations, but this was more characteristic of England than anywhere else, for reasons having to do with the greater independence of the English judiciary.

Again, it is important not to overemphasize the differences. Laissez-faire individualism was a powerful strain in all these legal systems at the turn of the century. Everywhere it met resistance, but in varying forms and degrees of strength. In France and Germany it was characterized by somewhat different views of man, society, and law from those which prevailed in England and the United States. Legal systems on the French and German model have imagined the human person as a free, self-determining individual, but also as a being defined in part through his relations with others. The individual is envisioned, more than in our legal system, as situated within family and community; rights are viewed as inseparable from corresponding responsibilities; and liberty and equality are seen as coordinate with fraternity. Personal values are regarded as higher than social values, but as rooted in them. This view of the world pervades court decisions, statutes, social programs, and constitutional texts.

For example, the West German Constitution (Basic Law) of 1949, with deliberate intent to correct for the gross distortions of the twelve-year Reich, gives primacy in Article 1 to the protection of human dignity. Then, in the following five articles, it expressly protects individual liberty, privacy, equality (including sexual equality), freedom of religion, freedom of expression, and marriage and the family. The very words "liberty" and "equality" resonate quite differently within the context of a twentieth-century document establishing a social welfare state, than within the eighteenth-century American Constitution. Interestingly, the explicit

protection given to a variety of competing, and sometimes conflicting, ideals seems to encourage the Federal Constitutional Court to
keep all of them in mind. Far from involving the court in hopeless
contradictions, these internal stresses in the constitutional structure appear to play a role in maintaining a constructive tension
among the parts. Judicial statements like the following are not
uncommon: "The concept of man in the Basic Law is not that of
an isolated sovereign individual; rather the Basic Law has decided
in favor of a relationship between individual and community in
the sense of a person's dependence on and commitment to the
community, without infringing upon a person's individual
value."[64]

In American constitutional law, on the other hand, the expressed rights to individual liberty and equal treatment are dominant. Though family protection notions are on occasion strongly
put forward through judicial interpretation, they are often forgotten or submerged, and the conflicts between them and the expressed values are seldom fully explored.[65] The West German Basic Law seems on the whole better adapted to ensure that no one
ideal will achieve undue prominence, as well as that none will be
unduly obscured. A similar situation obtains in France. The
French Declaration of the Rights of Man and the Citizen of 1789
made no reference to the family. The Preamble to the 1946 Constitution, however, provides that "The nation ensures to the individual and the family the conditions necessary to their development."[66] Both the Declaration of 1789, with its liberty, equality,
and fraternity, and the 1946 Preamble, with its family protection
language, are expressly incorporated in the Preamble to the current French Constitution.[67]

FAMILY POLICY

At this point I would like to draw out another, quite different but
still specifically legal strand that has to be part of any explanation
of why the continental countries and the United States diverge in
their approaches to the subjects with which we have been concerned here. The presence of specific family protection language in
many European constitutions is of a piece with the existence in

continental countries of explicit national family policy. In the United States, we have no counterpart to European cabinet ministers charged with responsibility for family affairs. Nor do we have mandatory national programs of maternity benefits and child care, or meaningful subsidies for families with children. We also lack those networks of local and national private or semiprivate organizations called family associations that exert quite a powerful influence on family policy in many countries. This does not mean that American society is anti-family, or that continental countries are particularly pro-family or pro-child. It does not even mean that we do not have a family policy. What it does mean is that our family policy is implicit, contained in the details of tax law, employment law, pension and insurance law, social welfare and social security law, and so on. Because it is implicit, it is largely unexamined, and its implications for family life are insufficiently aired and discussed.

Most European family policies and programs were originally established as a matter of population policy, and are maintained in part because of concern about declining birth rates. But their origins are of little import. As Daniel Lev has written, "In the nature of legal systems, concepts and structures developed in one age carry over as myth thereafter, transforming what once were straightforward matters of interest and power into principles and habits."[68] Family policy, once in place for whatever reason, makes a difference, as Daniel Patrick Moynihan, and Alva Myrdal before him have so persuasively argued.[69] Never mind that family policy may pursue one object in one country and quite a different one in another, or that in a single country it may be replete with internal contradictions. Symbolism is important. For instance, our tax deductions for children—apart from not helping the poorest families and not keeping up with inflation—are not the same as direct grants to families with children. Perhaps we would not wish to imitate France, which awards a "medal of the French family" to persons who have raised large families in an exemplary fashion— bronze for four or five, silver for six or seven, and gold for eight or more children.[70] But such gestures do communicate that society values child raising, and they may help to maintain an atmosphere that fosters other more tangible kinds of recognition. The mere existence of family policy—and of constitutional family protection language—helps to keep families, children, and therefore the future of the society constantly in the consciousness of the public and of government officials. The absence of such highly visible public symbols in the United States inevitably contributes to the impoverishment of political discourse about issues of vital national concern.

Yet another legal difference between the treatment of economic dependency in the United States and continental Europe concerns the broader social welfare context of family policy. This is too vast a subject to treat adequately here, but a comparatist may note that the birth and early development of the welfare state was less traumatic on the Continent than in the United States owing, to no small extent, to the fact that courts in European countries did not have the power to strike down statutes as unconstitutional. The social legislation of late nineteenth-century France and Germany encountered no such obstacles as the United States Supreme Court and state supreme courts posed to similar American measures. Throughout Western Europe today it is taken for granted that governments are responsible for public welfare; that they insure health, employment, and retirement; and that they will do so at more than minimal levels. The major European political parties of both right and left are in little practical disagreement on these points, even in countries where these goals are not immediately attainable.[71]

A comparative survey of social welfare law is not simply a matter of looking at the percentages of gross national product devoted to social expenditures or the total value of cash and in-kind transfers. It is also important to consider the kinds of messages welfare programs communicate about various sorts of economic dependency. The United States, for example, has a reasonably comprehensive program of social assistance for the needy, but its social expenditures are more heavily concentrated on the elderly, and less on children, than in most other countries.[72] Also in contrast to most other industrial democracies, with their broad range of family assistance programs, social assistance in the United States is, with rare exceptions, individual assistance. This emphasis on the individual in social welfare is, as Senator Moynihan has pointed out, "almost uniquely American."[73] Social assistance programs differ, too, in whether they appear to be rewarding the assumption or abandonment of personal responsibility, and whether they are designed and implemented in a spirit of respect for and solidarity with fellow human beings in need, or grudgingly and with contempt for the recipients.

The size and relative homogeneity of a country's population seem to have a great deal to do with the messages conveyed in the funding, design, and street-level administration of social assistance programs and their acceptance by the public. In the United States, more than in smaller, less heterogeneous countries, debate rages over whether public aid shores up families or erodes their capacity for self help, whether it really helps the needy or seals them into dependency. It is true that we know remarkably little about what kinds of state intervention help or hurt families and family members, and that laws, programs, and policies meant to strengthen families often seem to produce the opposite effects from those intended. Our society thinks of itself as generous. The Marshall Plan, among other things, stands as testimony that this image of ourselves is not unfounded. Across the American political spectrum the view is widely shared that society ought to assist the "truly needy." At the same time, however, the belief that many of the poor are not needy or deserving of aid is widespread. With respect to the large proportion of children among the poor, our seeming indifference is particularly puzzling, considering the obvious common interest we have in the human capital they represent.

Once again, it was Tocqueville who saw that the same forces that were fostering the rise of the individual would make it hard for modern societies to provide for the future, to discern long-range goals, and implement long-term policies. He speculated that when the links between generations and the ties between blood and soil were finally broken, a certain carelessness about the future would appear:[74] "Not only does democracy make men forget their ancestors, but it also clouds their view of their descendants and isolates them from their contemporaries. Each man is forever thrown back on himself alone, and there is danger that he may be shut up in the solitude of his own heart."[75] Tocqueville knew that this inclination to concentrate on the self and on the present would have political consequences. In countries where skepticism and democracy coexist, he wrote, men can "easily fall back into a complete and brutish indifference about the future," an attitude, as he said, "all too well suited to certain propensities of human nature."[76] Because of all the pressures on individuals to consider only their immediate needs and desires, Tocqueville realized that long-range planning would always pose serious problems for democratic societies. He maintained, therefore, that it was the role of philosophers in such societies to constantly endeavor to direct the eyes of the citizenry to long-term goals, and of statesmen to "study means to give men back that interest in the future which neither religion nor social conditions any longer inspire."[77]

THE CONTINUING CONVERSATION

In attempting to elucidate the puzzles of American uniqueness posed at the outset of this book, I have been pursuing only certain aspects of the problem. The justification for my emphasis on ideas, and especially on ideas about law, is that their role in explaining the distinctiveness of American law on the subjects discussed here has been so little noted. But of course law cannot be neatly separated from many other important nonlegal factors. The same kinds of difficulties that attend any attempt to trace the role that ideas may have had in the making of American law also burden any speculation about the role that law might play in affecting behavior and ideas. No one can chart with confidence the ways in which law, customs, new lines of behavior, ideas about law, and ideas about morality reciprocally influence each other. Law is importantly shaped by its surrounding culture, but it seems to have only a limited capacity to influence the culture in its turn. Ideas in legal texts migrate into other contexts, connect there with other ideas, and are sometimes internalized. The implementation (or lack thereof) of laws and programs no doubt creates expectations and influences action. But often this happens in such complex ways as to be unpredictable. The effects of law, if they can be discerned at all, are frequently quite different from what was expected or intended.

In part this is because only the most elementary legal information reaches the public, and this almost always in a slightly inaccurate form.[78] Relayed through lawyers, newspapers, magazines, television, radio, or by family and friends, what comes through is frequently only a sort of cartoon of the law in question. Even a lawyer is apt to have an inaccurate understanding of a field in which he is not a specialist. (One can test this by asking people what they think will happen to their property if they die without leaving wills, or what they think a person's legal name is, or any number of other simple legal questions related to everyday life.)

Leaving these problems of communication aside, twentieth-century experience with totalitarianism has made us rightly wary of the classical view that a purpose of law is to promote virtue. Who is to define virtue? we moderns must ask. But even so, there is no escape from the fact that, willy-nilly, law performs a pedagog-ical role. It contributes in a modest but not a trivial way to that framework of beliefs and feelings within which even our notions of self-interest are conceived. Thus the impossibility of identifying a single widely shared notion of virtue or the common good in modern societies does not mean that modern law can remain reso-lutely neutral on all controversial questions involving moral issues. Indeed, neutral is the one thing it cannot be, for refusing to take a moral position is a moral stand in itself. This is a matter of particu-lar concern in a pluralistic, secular society like that of the United States, where the mystic chords of memory that Lincoln evoked are now barely audible. A people that lacks a common religion, history, or customs is apt to regard law, especially criminal law and constitutional law, as an expression and source of common values. But at the same time that law is increasingly treated as a value-carrier, there is an almost total lack of agreement about how and where the values it carries are to be discovered. In this predica-ment it is only natural that ideas of law as embodying a social dialogue should come to have a special appeal.[79]

These new legal ideas track the efforts of several contemporary philosophers to escape from the quarrel between the ancients and the moderns by recasting its terms. Many have abandoned that part of the Enlightenment program which was the development of a rational, secular basis for morality. They have tended to replace the search for "truth" or "morality" or "values" with attention to the search itself. Thus we find increased interest, even among legal theorists, in what Jürgen Habermas describes as "communicative action," or what Alasdair MacIntyre calls the process of "socially embodied argument."[80] As we saw in the discussions of abortion and divorce law, such social conversation is not an orderly, structured process. It can be carried on at many levels and in many places. It is not always cordial and is often marked by misunderstandings. Still, MacIntyre maintains the process is a sign of health and vigor in society: "When a tradition is in good order it is always partially constituted by an argument about the goods the pursuit of which gives to that tradition its particular point and purpose."[81] This increased attention to social dialogue fits well with the Aristotelian insight that by our doing and our ways of knowing we make ourselves what we are. The reappropriation of Aristotle in turn leads to a new appreciation of the role of imagination in determining what we will become as individuals and as a society. And just as attention to the process of human knowing puts the quarrel between classical and modern political theory in a different perspective, so awareness of the power of imagination sheds new light on the quarrel that Plato began between poetry and philosophy.

The eventual implications for legal theory of a slow and painstaking attempt at reconstruction of moral philosophy will long be unclear. But it does not seem too soon to say that although modern law cannot establish or enforce a single vision of virtue, it can play its part in promoting the potentially self-correcting processes of dialogue and dialectic. Legal scholars such as James B. White are clearly wise to begin to look at law as constitutive rhetoric. Those views of law that have been so fashionable within the American legal profession since the late nineteenth century—that moral questions are out of bounds, and that the task of law is to adapt itself to behavior—impoverish discussion and diminish us. Such attitudes render insight and self-correction less likely to occur, and lend themselves to perpetuation of long cycles of decline. At worst they are counselors of nihilism and despair.

In this light, then, one can appreciate the legal treatment of divorce and abortion in the continental countries. In their current approaches to these problems, which may at first seem to be mere political compromises, satisfactory to no one and shot through with inconsistencies, a conversation is going on about the right way to live. The surveys in Chapters 1 and 2 showed that all over Western Europe the predominant choice of law reformers has been to maintain a widely shared ideal in the law—in the one case, the value of developing life, and in the other, responsibility in personal relationships—while accommodating the opinions and behavior of those who do not share or cannot live up to the ideal. Prudent attention was given in both cases to whether the new laws could be enforced, and, if so, whether they could be applied equitably. In their use of law-making as an occasion for dialogue, as in their attempts to preserve a sense of responsibility and social context along with regard for individuals and their rights, contemporary civil law systems differ from their Anglo-American counterparts. They also contrast with the other extreme represented by the Soviet model, where the individual is subordinated to the community (an abstract entity identified with the state), and law is regarded as a didactic instrument in the service of the state.

As with law in general, so it is with laws affecting families, though the political importance of families—so obvious and central to Plato, Rousseau, and Tocqueville—is today almost always ignored. The present legal ordering of the family is composed of the accumulated accidents and inventions of the past. We are now in the process of adding a layer that will reflect the circumstances of our own time and whatever intelligence we are able to bring to bear. But when one tries to view law as one of the ways in which societies constitute themselves, one is vividly reminded of Tocqueville's observation that laws are far less important than those habitual and intellectual attitudes which he called the mores.[82] The extent to which law can influence the ways people think, act, and feel, depends, I suspect, to a great extent on whether it is in harmony with other ways in which a society perceives reality—its art, science, literature, religion, history, and mass media. It is not likely that any law passed in Rome in the third century A.D. could have had much of an effect on mores in the coming era of plagues, invasions, and civil war. And there are those who say that the new dark ages are already upon us.[83] At the same time, others claim that Americans have a half-forgotten second language of generosity and community, which here and there breaks through the first language of self-fulfillment and gives rise to the hope that as a nation we might still have the will, the charity, the vocabulary, and the vision to imagine a better way to live.[84] But, alas, a language like any other habit is strengthened by practice and atrophies through disuse.

What is to be done? Because law is interpretive, we need to make the effort to understand what the totality of our legal regulations relating to family life is saying about our society and the way we view families, individuals, human life, dependency, and neediness in all its forms. Because law is also constitutive, it is incumbent on us to be attentive, intelligent, reasonable, and responsible in the "stories we tell," the "symbols we deploy," and the "visions we project."[85] Because the role of law in the constitution of culture is so much more limited than that of the mores, it also behooves lawmakers to be solicitous of, or at least to try to avoid damaging groups such as families, churches, and local communities where values are formed, maintained, and transmitted. Comparative law does not provide blueprints or solutions. But awareness of foreign experiences does lead to the kind of self-understanding that constitutes a necessary first step on the way toward working out our own approaches to our own problems.

These observations about the limits of law bring me back, finally, to Plato's Laws. At the end of the dialogue, when the discussion among the three elderly travelers comes to a close, the Athenian Stranger points out that their conversation about law has come back once again to education and nurture.[86] As night falls, the Spartan and the Cretan implore their new friend to stay and help with the founding of the new city. Without him, they say, they will have to give up the whole undertaking. But the Stranger does not respond, and Plato's last dialogue ends with a resonating silence. There are no easy recipes for law making in a real republic. It may be, as Socrates enigmatically suggested elsewhere, that there are times when we need enchantments, inspiration, or poetry as much as we need philosophy.[87] If law is, among other things, the art of pursuing dignified living, of establishing meaning and constituting community, modern polities require artists worthy of these tasks. Search out these inspired persons, said Socrates in the *Phaedo,* in every corner of this vast country, and even in barbarian lands, for truly, no task is more important.[88]

APPENDIXES

NOTES

INDEX

APPENDIX A

COUNTRIES PERMITTING
ABORTION FOR CAUSE

Canada

The Canadian Criminal Code makes abortion a criminal offense except where a therapeutic abortion committee of three doctors in an approved hospital has certified that continuation of the pregnancy would be likely to endanger the life or health of the pregnant woman: Canadian Criminal Code Section 251, R.S.C., as amended in 1969. In a 1975 case the Supreme Court of Canada left open the possibility that the defense of necessity could be proved in a criminal prosecution for an abortion not approved by such a committee: *Morgentaler v. The Queen* (1975) 53 D.L.R. (3d) 161. A later Quebec Court of Appeal decision indicates that evidence of less than an immediate risk to the pregnant woman's health may be accepted to prove "necessity": *Regina v. Morgentaler* (1976) 64 *Dominion Law Reports* (3d) 718. There are said to be great variations in the availability of abortion throughout Canada: Margaret Somerville, "Reflections on Canadian Abortion Law," 31 *University of Toronto Law Journal* 1, 9 (1981); Linda Long, "The Abortion Issue: An Overview," 23 *Alberta Law Review* 453, 473 (1985).

Finland

Finnish abortion law was amended in 1970 to permit abortions on a variety of grounds. Stating that abortions "must be performed at the earliest possible stage of pregnancy," the 1970 law listed the following situations where termination is allowed through the sixteenth week: danger to the life or health of the woman; likelihood the child would be born with a serious disease or defect; pregnancy resulting from a duly reported criminal offense against the woman; severe impairment of a parent's ability to take care of a child; a serious strain on the woman in relation to her and her family's general living conditions in consequence of the birth or care of a child; age of the woman at the time of conception under seventeen or over forty; or the case of a woman who has already given birth to four children. Abortion is permitted up to the twentieth week where "special reasons apply" or where the woman was under seventeen at the time of conception. Thereafter abortion is permitted only on grounds relating to the woman's health. In most cases the recommendation of two physicians or the State Medical Board is required. A 1978 amendment reduced the period during which abortions on grounds unrelated to the physical health of the woman are permitted from sixteen weeks to twelve, and in 1986 the period during which abortion of a seriously defective fetus is permitted was extended to twenty-four weeks.

Finnish Law No. 239 of 24 March 1970, as amended by Law No. 564 of 14 July 1978, is translated in 21 *International Digest of Health Legislation* 699 (1970) (hereafter *I.D.H.L.*) and 30 *I.D.H.L.* 30 (1979).

France

Since 1975 abortion has been available in France in cases of "necessity." In the first ten weeks the necessity requirement is satisfied if the pregnant woman considers herself "in distress," provided she undergoes mandatory counseling and (except in cases of emergency) observes waiting periods of one week from the date of her original request and two days from the date of counseling. After ten weeks abortion is available only when two physicians certify that the pregnancy poses a serious danger to the woman's health or that the child is likely to be born with a serious disease or defect.

French Law No. 75-17 of 17 January 1975 (*Journal officiel,* hereafter *J.O.,* Jan. 18, 1975, p. 739), re-enacted and amended by Law No. 79-1204 of 31 December 1979, *J.O.* Jan. 1, 1980, p. 3, is set forth in relevant part in Appendix C. See also pp. 15–19 above.

West Germany

Under the West German Criminal Code since 1976, abortion after implantation of the fertilized ovum has been illegal except when a doctor (who is not performing the abortion) confirms the pregnancy poses a serious danger to the life or physical or mental health of the pregnant woman, which cannot be averted any other way the woman can reasonably be expected to bear. In making this determination, the doctor may consider the "present and future living conditions" of the woman. In addition, abortion is permitted through the twenty-second week if a doctor (who is not performing the abortion) confirms the child is likely to be born with such a severe defect that the woman cannot reasonably be expected to continue with the pregnancy, and through the twelfth week if a doctor (who is not performing the abortion) confirms the pregnancy resulted from an illegal act against the woman or if pregnancy places her in a situation of serious hardship that cannot be averted any other way. Except in emergencies, at least three days must elapse after a mandatory counseling session in which the pregnant woman must be advised of services available to her, especially ones that would facilitate continuation of the pregnancy. Even when abortion is not otherwise exempt from punishment, a hardship clause gives the court discretion to suspend punishment for the woman if she was in a situation of extraordinary distress.

West German Criminal Code Sections 218 through 219c, as amended by Fifteenth Statute to Reform the Penal Law of May 18, 1976 (Bundesgesetzblatt I, 1213) is translated in 27 *I.D.H.L.* 562 (1976). See also pp. 25–33 above.

Iceland

Since 1975 abortion in early pregnancy has been available on a wide variety of grounds. In addition to situations where two physicians certify that the pregnancy poses a danger to the woman's physical or mental health, or has resulted from a criminal act, or is likely to result in the birth of a child with a serious defect, the 1975 statute lists a number of "social reasons." These social factors must be certified by a physician and a social worker. They are defined as factors beyond the control of the pregnant woman, which make the pregnancy and the advent of a child "too difficult for the woman and her close family." Such factors may include but are not limited to: difficulties arising from the birth of many children at short intervals, the poor health of family members, or the youth or mental incapacity of the pregnant woman. The statute provides that "an abortion shall be performed as early as possible and preferably before the end of the twelfth week of pregnancy." Abortions after the sixteenth week are forbidden unless a medical committee certifies that the life and health of the woman are in serious danger or that the child is likely to be born with defects or damage. Any woman who applies for an abortion is required to have counseling about what social assistance is available to her, and any woman who has an abortion must be given guidance about contraceptives before she leaves the hospital and must return later for a medical examination and "a conversation."

Icelandic Law No. 25/1975 of 27 May 1975 is translated in *Annual Review of Population Law 1976* (1977), 53 (hereafter *A.R.P.L.*).

Italy

Since 1978 abortion has been available during the first ninety days of pregnancy if the woman, after counseling and a seven-day waiting period, requests it because of serious danger to her physical or mental health in view of her "state of health, [her] economic, social, or family circumstances, the circumstances in which conception occurred, or the probability that the child would be born with abnormalities or malformations." After ninety days abortions may be performed only when a physician certifies that the pregnancy constitutes a serious danger to the woman's life or physical or mental health. Where it is "possible" that the fetus may be viable, abortion is permitted only to save the life of the woman and the physician must take "any appropriate action" to save the life of the fetus.

Italian Law No. 194 of 22 May 1978 on the Social Protection of Motherhood and the Voluntary Termination of Pregnancy is translated in 29 *I.D.H.L.* 589 (1978). See also note 51, pp. 163–64 below.

Luxembourg

Since 1978 abortion is permitted during the first twelve weeks of pregnancy after consultation and a one-week waiting period, if a physician certifies that the pregnancy or the living conditions that would result from the birth are likely to put the woman's mental or physical health at risk, or that the child is likely to be born with a serious defect, or that the pregnancy is likely to have resulted from rape. Thereafter, a pregnancy may be terminated only if two physicians certify to a serious threat to the life or health of the pregnant woman or the unborn child.

Luxembourgeois Law of 15 November 1978, concerning Sex Education, Prevention of Clandestine Abortion, and Regulation of the Voluntary Interruption of Pregnancy, is translated in *A.R.P.L. 1978* (1979), 22.

The Netherlands

Under the 1981 abortion statute, abortion is permitted up to viability but only if the woman finds herself in distress and if her situation leaves her no other choice. There is a five-day waiting period. Administrative regulations authorized by the statute require that the pregnant woman be furnished with "information regarding ways of dealing with her distressed situation other than termination of pregnancy." These regulations are supposed to ensure that "the physician is satisfied that the woman has submitted and upheld her request of her own free will, after careful consideration and in full awareness of her responsibilities towards the unborn child." Finally, the regulations are to try to assure that physicians will perform abortions only if they consider them "justifiable."

The Netherlands Law of 1 May 1981 on the Termination of Pregnancy is translated in *A.R.P.L. 1981* (1982), 57 and 32 *I.D.H.L.* 442 (1981).

Portugal

Since 1984 criminal penalties for abortion do not apply in the following situations: if the abortion is performed during the first twelve weeks in cases of rape or where the pregnancy poses a risk of death or serious damage to the physical or mental health of the woman; if it is performed during the first sixteen weeks provided that it is likely the child would be born with a serious disease or defect; and at any time if it is the sole means of eliminating a risk of death or serious permanent damage to the physical or mental health of the woman. The existence of these circumstances must be certified by a physician, other than the one performing the abortion, and a three-day waiting period is required except in cases of emergency.

Portuguese Law No. 6184 of 11 May 1984 is translated in 35 *I.D.H.L.* 768 (1984).

Spain

In 1985, the Spanish Constitutional Court held that a liberal abortion law passed in 1983 would have to be modified to pass constitutional muster. Subsequently the Spanish Penal Code was amended to exempt from criminal punishment abortions performed by a physician when a second physician certifies that the procedure is necessary "to avert a serious risk to the physical or mental health of the pregnant woman"; or where the pregnancy is a result of rape (duly reported) and the abortion is performed within the first twelve weeks of pregnancy; or where two physicians (other than the one performing the abortion) certify it is likely the fetus will be born with severe physical or mental defects, and the abortion is performed within the first twenty-two weeks of pregnancy.

Spanish Penal Code Art. 417 *bis,* as amended by Organic Law 9/1985 of July 5, 1985, is translated in 36 *I.D.H.L.* 614–15 (1985). See also pp. 38–39 above.

Switzerland

Abortion is illegal under the federal criminal code except when two physicians certify that the pregnancy is likely to endanger the woman's life or pose a lasting serious danger to her health, and that these dangers cannot be averted in any other way. The provisions of the criminal code have not been changed since 1942, but are interpreted liberally in some cantons and quite restrictively in others. Until the recent wave of change in abortion law, this Swiss statute was one of the most liberal in Western Europe. Pregnant women of means from other countries frequently traveled to the Swiss cantons where "health" was interpreted broadly in order to have safe, legal abortions. Starting in the 1970s there were many attempts to reformulate Swiss abortion law along the lines of the newer abortion legislation in other West European countries, but so far all have been defeated.

See the Swiss Criminal Code, Articles 118–121.

United Kingdom (except Northern Ireland)

Under the Offenses Against the Person Act of 1861, abortion is a crime in the United Kingdom if it is performed "unlawfully." The Abortion Act of 1967 (which is in effect in England, Scotland, and Wales) provides that an abortion is "lawful" if two physicians in good faith certify that the pregnancy poses a risk to the life or physical or mental health of the pregnant woman or any existing children of her family "greater than if the pregnancy were terminated," or that the child would be likely to be born seriously handicapped. In assessing the risk to the health of the woman and her existing children, the certifying physicians may take account of the woman's "actual or reasonably foreseeable environment." The 1967 Act does not affect the provisions of the Infant Life (Preservation) Act 1929 which makes it a criminal offense to cause the death of an unborn child capable of being born alive, except where this is done to save the life of the mother. Viability for purposes of this statute has been interpreted to mean a fetal age of twenty-eight weeks.

The Abortion Act 1967 is set forth in full in *Survey of Laws on Fertility Control* 92 (U.N. Fund for Population Activities, 1979).

APPENDIX B

COUNTRIES PERMITTING ABORTION ON DEMAND

Austria

Abortion is a criminal offense, but since 1974 it is exempt from punishment when performed by a physician during the first three months of pregnancy after a medical consultation; and thereafter when necessary to avert a serious danger to the life or physical or mental health of the pregnant woman which could not be averted any other way, or when it is likely the child would be born with a serious defect, or when the woman became pregnant when under fourteen years of age.

The Austrian Federal Law of 23 January 1974 is translated in 26 *International Digest of Health Legislation* 226 (1975) (hereafter *I.D.H.L.*) and *Annual Review of Population Law 1975* (1976), 47 (hereafter *A.R.P.L.*). It was upheld by the Austrian Constitutional Court in a decision of Oct. 11, 1974, which appears in Mauro Cappelletti and William Cohen, *Comparative Constitutional Law* (Indianapolis: Bobbs-Merrill, 1979), 615.

Denmark

Since 1973 the Danish law states that a woman is "entitled to undergo an abortion provided that the procedure can be performed during the first twelve weeks of pregnancy," providing that the woman has been informed of the availability of assistance in continuing the pregnancy to term and in caring for the child after the birth, as well as of the nature and risks of the abortion procedure. After the twelfth week abortion is available upon authorization by a special committee in the following cases: if the woman's health is at risk in view of existing physical or mental infirmity or "as a consequence of other aspects of the conditions under which she is living"; if the pregnancy resulted from certain criminal offenses; if it is likely the child would be afflicted with a serious disorder; if the woman is incapable of giving proper care to a child; or, if under all the circumstances of the woman and her family, the pregnancy or birth or care of a child would "constitite a serious burden to the woman, which cannot otherwise be averted." Abortion is available after the twelfth week without special authorization if necessary to avert a risk to the woman's life or a serious risk of a medical nature to her physical or mental health.

Danish Law No. 350 of 13 June 1973 on the termination of pregnancy is translated in 24 *I.D.H.L.* 773 (1973). It was amended by Law No. 254 of 12 June 1975, translated in 27 *I.D.H.L.* 113 (1976).

Greece

In 1986 Greece moved from permitting early abortions only on the so-called hard grounds, to a system of elective abortion during the first twelve weeks of pregnancy. After the first trimester, abortion can be obtained through the twenty-fourth week for medical reasons relating to the physical or mental health of the pregnant woman or the development of the fetus and through the nineteenth week where the pregnancy resulted from a criminal act. Advertisement of abortifacients or abortion services (except information supplied in family planning centers) remains a criminal offense. The law that was superseded, which had been adopted in 1978, had itself represented a liberalization of a stricter provision of former Article 304 of the Greek Penal Code. Greece, 14 *People* 35 (1987).

Norway

In Norway a 1978 law permits abortion when a pregnant woman, who, after having been offered information and guidance, "considers that she still is unable to take the pregnancy to term . . . shall personally reach a final decision to terminate the pregnancy, provided that the operation may be performed before the end of the twelfth week of pregnancy and there are no serious medical arguments weighing against it." After the twelfth week an abortion may be performed, when authorized by a committee, under the following circumstances: if pregnancy, birth, or child care would place "an unreasonable strain upon the physical or mental health of the woman" or would place her "in difficult circumstances"; if there is a major risk the child would suffer from a serious defect; if the woman became pregnant as a result of certain criminal acts; or if the woman is severely mentally ill or retarded. The committee, in evaluating a request on these grounds, is directed to give major consideration to the woman's own assessment of her situation, and is advised that "the conditions for authorizing a pregnancy termination shall become more stringent as the duration of the pregnancy increases." After the eighteenth week the law provides that a pregnancy may not be terminated "unless there are particularly important grounds for doing so." If there is reason to assume the fetus is viable, authorization for abortion may not be granted. The first section of the 1978 law contains the following statement of principle:

> Society shall ensure as far as is possible that all children enjoy conditions for a secure upbringing. As part of this task, society shall ensure that all persons receive ethical guidance, sex education, information on matters of communal living, and family planning facilities, in order to create a responsible attitude to such matters so that the number of pregnancy terminations is as low as possible.

The 1978 law amended a 1975 law which permitted abortions for cause only, even in the first trimester.

Norwegian Law No. 66 of 16 June 1978, amending Law No. 50 of 13 June 1975 on the termination of pregnancy, is translated in 30 *I.D.H.L.* 126–28 (1979). The 1975 law is translated in 27 *I.D.H.L.* 594 (1976).

Sweden

Under the 1974 Swedish abortion law, abortion is available upon the pregnant woman's request during the first eighteen weeks of pregnancy if there are no medical contraindications. After the twelfth week a session with a social worker is required. After the eighteenth week an abortion can be performed only if authorized by the National Board of Health and Welfare. Such authorization can be granted only if there are "substantial grounds justifying abortion" and not at all if there are grounds for assuming the fetus is viable, unless the pregnancy is found by the board to seriously endanger the woman's life or health.

Swedish Abortion Law (No. 595) of 14 June 1974, is translated in 25 *I.D.H.L.* 618 (1974). See also pp. 22–23 above.

United States

Since the Supreme Court decision in *Roe v. Wade*, 410 U.S. 113 (1973), abortion has been available on the request of the pregnant woman until viability, subject only to regulation after the end of the first trimester in the interest of protecting the health of the woman. A state law requiring second trimester abortions to be performed in a hospital was held unconstitutional in *Planned Parenthood Association v. Ashcroft,* 462 U.S. 476 (1983), calling into question whether any significant regulation prior to viability would pass constitutional muster. After viability, which the Supreme Court has estimated as occurring between twenty-four and twenty-eight weeks, state regulation to protect the fetus is not constitutionally required but is permitted, except where abortion is necessary to "preserve the life or health of the mother." *Roe v. Wade,* 410 U.S. 113, 164 (1973). However, state laws attempting to require doctors performing abortions to try to preserve the life of a viable fetus were struck down in *Colautti v. Franklin,* 439 U.S. 379 (1979), and *Thornburgh v. American College of Obstetricians and Gynecologists,* 54 *Law Week* 4618 (1986), casting doubt on the extent to which state regulation in the interest of the fetus even in late pregnancy will be upheld. See also pp. 22–24, 33–39 above.

APPENDIX C

THE FRENCH ABORTION LAW OF 1975

Excerpts from Law No. 75-17 of 17 January 1975, concerning voluntary termination of pregnancy, as amended by Law No. 79-1204 of 31 December 1979. (The 1979 amendments are in brackets. The translation is mine.)

1. The law guarantees the respect of every human being from the commencement of life. There shall be no derogation from this principle except in cases of necessity and under the conditions laid down by this law.

[The teaching of this principle and its consequences, the provision of information on the problems of life and of national and international demography, the education towards responsibility, the acceptance of the child in society, and family-oriented policy, are national obligations. The State, with the co-operation of local authorities, implements these obligations and supports initiatives towards these ends.]

13. The voluntary termination of pregnancy must under no circumstances constitute a means of birth control. In this connection, the government shall take all the measures necessary to promote information on birth control on as wide a scale as possible, notably by the universal establishment, within maternal and child care centers, of family planning or education centers, and by the utilization of all communications media.

[The education and practical training of physicians, midwives, and nurses (male and female) shall include instruction concerning contraception.]

Voluntary Termination of Pregnancy Performed
before the End of the Tenth Week

Article L. 162-1. A pregnant woman whose condition places her in a situation of distress may make a request to a physician for the termination of her pregnancy. The termination may be performed only before the end of the tenth week of pregnancy.

Article L. 162-2. A voluntary termination of pregnancy may be performed only by a physician.

The procedure must be carried out only in a public or private hospital conforming to the provisions of Article L. 176.

[Article L. 162-3. A physician who has been approached by a woman with a view to the termination of her pregnancy is required at the time of her first visit, to:

(1) inform her of the medical risks to herself and to her future maternity; and of the biological seriousness of the operation requested by her;

(2) furnish her with an information folder, to be updated at least once every year, containing in particular:

(a) a reference to the provisions of Article 1 of Law No. 75-17 of 17 January, 1975 as well as to the provisions of Article L. 162-1 of this code, limiting the termination of pregnancy to those cases where the pregnant woman is by her condition placed in a situation of distress;

(b) a list of the rights, forms of assistance, and benefits guaranteed by law to families, mothers, including unmarried mothers, and their children, as well as of the possibilities offered by adoption of children to be born;

(c) a list and the addresses of the institutions referred to in Article L. 162-4 as well as of the associations and institutions capable of supplying the persons concerned with moral or material assistance; and

(d) a list and the addresses of establishments where voluntary terminations of pregnancies are performed.]

Article L. 162-4. A woman who considers herself to be placed in the situation referred to in Article L. 162-1 must, after completion of the formalities prescribed in Article L. 162-3, consult a family information, counseling, or advisory establishment, a family planning or education center, a social welfare service, or any other approved institution, which shall furnish her with a certificate to the effect that the consultation has taken place.

This consultation shall be in the form of a private interview during which the woman shall be provided with assistance and advice appropriate to her situation, as well as the necessary means to resolve the social problems posed [especially with a view to enabling her to keep her child. On this occasion she shall be supplied with the names and addresses of persons who, either as individuals or acting on behalf of organizations, may be able to provide moral or material assistance to women and couples facing problems of accepting or raising a child.

With the exception of public hospitals, the above consultations may not be undertaken inside establishments where voluntary terminations of pregnancies are performed.]

Wherever possible, both partners shall participate in the consultation and in the decision to be taken.

Article L. 162-5. Should the woman repeat her request for a pregnancy termination after the consultations referred to in Article L. 162-3 and L. 162-4, the physician must ask her to give written confirmation; he may not accept such confirmation before a period of one week has elapsed following the woman's initial request [except in cases where there is a risk that the period of ten weeks might be exceeded, the physician being the sole judge of the propriety of his decision. Moreover, this confirmation may not be given sooner than two days after the consultation provided for in Article L. 162-4, which time may be included in the period of one week provided for above.]

Voluntary Termination of Pregnancy Performed on Therapeutic Grounds

Article L. 162-12. A voluntary termination of pregnancy may be performed at any stage of gestation if two physicians certify, after an examination and discussion, that the continuation of the pregnancy is seriously endangering the woman's health or that there is a strong possibility that the unborn child is suffering from a particularly serious disease or condition considered as incurable at the time of the diagnosis.

One of the two physicians must be practicing his profession in a public or private hospital conforming to the provisions of Article L. 176, while the other must be entered on a list of experts registered with the Court of Cassation or a Court of Appeal.

NOTES

Introduction

1. John P. Dawson, *Unjust Enrichment: A Comparative Analysis* (Boston: Little, Brown, 1951), 111.

2. Sir Otto Kahn-Freund, "Comparative Law as an Academic Subject," 82 *Law Quarterly Review* 40, 41 (1966).

3. Interest in legal comparisons has been exhibited on occasion by philosophers and historians since antiquity, but systematic comparative legal studies began with the founding of the French Société de Législation Comparée (1869), the *Zeitschrift für vergleichende Rechtswissenschaft* (1878), and the English Society of Comparative Legislation (1898). Max Rheinstein, "Legal Systems: Comparative Law and Legal Systems," in *Gesammelte Schriften/Collected Works,* ed. H. Leser (Tübingen: J. C. B. Mohr, 1979), 239, 242.

4. So Hans-Georg Gadamer maintains in *Dialogue and Dialectic: Eight Hermeneutical Studies on Plato* (New Haven: Yale University Press, 1980), 71.

5. Thomas L. Pangle, *The Laws of Plato: Translated with Notes and an Interpretive Essay* (New York: Basic Books, 1980), 3.

6. "A god, stranger, a god—to say what is at any rate the most just thing. Among us Zeus, and among the Lacedaimonians . . . I think they declare that it's Apollo". Ibid., 624.

7. Ibid., 702.

8. Ibid., 386, 402.

9. Ibid., 375.

10. Ibid., 133–34.

11. Ibid., 951, 953.

12. See Leo Strauss, *The Argument and the Action of Plato's Laws* (Chicago: University of Chicago Press, 1975), 17; H.-G. Gadamer, *Dialogue and Dialectic,* 73. The question in *The Laws* is not about what kind of state is best in the abstract, as in *The Republic,* but about what state is best relative to circumstances.

13. Pangle, *The Laws of Plato,* 106.

14. Ibid., 110.

15. On this, even Hart and Devlin agree. See Lord Devlin, "Law, Democracy and Morality," 110 *University of Pennsylvania Law Review* 635, 638 (1962), and H. L. A. Hart, *Law, Liberty and Morality* (Stanford: Stanford University Press, 1963), 75.

16. Niklas Luhmann, 2 *Rechtssoziologie* 224–26 (Reinbeck/Hamburg: Rowohlt, 1972); Jean Carbonnier, "Variations sur la loi pédagogue," in *Società, Norme e Valori: Scritti in Onore di Renato Treves* (Milan: Giuffre, 1984). See also the essays in honor of Theodor Viehweg in *Rhetorische Rechtstheorie,* ed. Ottmar Ballweg and Thomas-Michael Seifert (Freiburg: Alber, 1982). The leading modern proponent of the idea that rhetoric is complementary to formal reasoning and is capable of leading to the discovery of truth was the Belgian legal philosopher, Chaim Perelman, author of *The New Rhetoric: A Treatise on Argumentation* (Notre Dame, Ind.: University of Notre Dame Press, 1969), and *The Realm of Rhetoric* (Notre Dame, Ind.: University of Notre Dame Press, 1982).

17. James Boyd White, "Law as Rhetoric, Rhetoric as Law: The Arts of Cultural and Communal Life," 52 *University of Chicago Law Review* 684 (1985). See also James Boyd White, *Heracles' Bow: Essays on the Rhetoric and Poetics of the Law* (Madison, Wis.: University of Wisconsin Press, 1985). Where White parts company with Plato, I believe, is in his view of the relationship of rhetoric to philosophy. It is implicit in his writing that rhetoric is not for him, as it was for Plato and Aristotle, properly subordinate to and in the service of philosophy and the art of statesmanship.

18. Clifford Geertz, *Local Knowledge: Further Essays in Interpretive Anthropology* (New York: Basic Books, 1983), 175.

19. Ibid., 173.

20. Ibid., 175.

21. J. B. White, "Law as Rhetoric," 691.

22. Ibid., 699.

1. Abortion Law

1. See, for example, the French Civil Code, former Art. 213 ("The husband owes protection to his wife, the wife obedience to her husband"); and Art. 371 ("A child of any age owes honor and respect to his father and mother").

2. See the French Civil Code, Art. 213 ("The spouses together provide the moral and material direction of the family"); West German Civil Code, Section 1356(1) ("The spouses regulate the running of the household by mutual agreement").

3. "A child may not be subjected to corporal punishment or other injurious or humiliating treatment," Swedish Författningssamling 1979: 122, translated and discussed by Dennis Alan Olson, "The Swedish Ban of Corporal Pun-

ishment," 1984 *Brigham Young University Law Review* 447. There are no criminal sanctions for violating this 1979 law, so long as the conduct does not amount to child abuse. Finland adopted a similar statute in 1983.

4. See the comparative surveys in Mary Ann Glendon, *State, Law and Family: Family Law in Transition in the United States and Western Europe* (Amsterdam: North Holland Publishing Co., 1977) and Mary Ann Glendon, *The New Family and the New Property* (Toronto: Butterworths, 1981).

5. Gilbert Y. Steiner, *The Futility of Family Policy* (Washington, D.C.: Brookings Institution, 1981), 51.

6. For the history of the prior laws, see Evert Ketting and Philip van Praag, *Schwangerschaftsabbruch: Gesetz und Praxis im internationalen Vergleich* (Tübingen: DGVT, 1985) where discussions of the current abortion laws of nine countries are prefaced, country by country, with descriptions of their historical background. See also, for history of abortion laws in the United States, Kristin Luker, *Abortion and the Politics of Motherhood* (Berkeley: University of California Press, 1984), 11–39.

7. Reform of the abortion laws occurred in Austria, Canada, Denmark, Finland, France, West Germany, Greece, Iceland, Italy, Luxembourg, the Netherlands, Norway, Portugal, Spain, Sweden, United Kingdom, and the United States. There has been no recent fundamental change in Belgium, Ireland, or Switzerland. See Appendixes A and B.

8. John T. Noonan, *A Private Choice: Abortion in America in the Seventies* (New York: The Free Press, 1979), 38.

9. K. Luker, *Abortion and the Politics of Motherhood,* 40–55.

10. The unreported decision is described in Note, "Declaratory Relief in the Criminal Law," 80 *Harvard Law Review* 1490 (1967).

11. K. Luker, *Abortion and the Politics of Motherhood,* 262–65.

12. Belgian Penal Code, Sections 350–53. Belgian case law treats abortion as justified by "necessity" when three doctors certify that the pregnancy constitutes an immediate serious threat to the health of the pregnant woman. Marie-Thérèse Meulders-Klein, "Considérations sur les problèmes juridiques de l'avortement," 31 *Annales de Droit* 425, 493 (1971).

The situation in Ireland is not entirely clear. It is generally thought that, where the life of the pregnant woman is in immediate danger, necessity would be a defense to a criminal prosecution under the statute which forbids anyone to "unlawfully" procure or perform an abortion, but no Irish court has ruled on this point. John A. Quinlan, "The Right to Life of the Unborn—An Assessment of the Eighth Amendment to the Irish Constitution," 1984 *Brigham Young University Law Review* 371, 372, 375. The 1983 "pro-life" amendment to the Irish Constitution puts the mother's right to life on an equal basis with that of the fetus: "The State acknowledges the right to life of the unborn and, with due regard to the equal right to life of the mother, guarantees in its laws to respect, and, as far as practicable, by its laws to defend and vindicate that right." Ibid., 385.

13. The middle-range countries are Canada, Finland, France, West Germany, Iceland, Italy, Luxembourg, the Netherlands, Portugal, Spain, Switzerland, and the United Kingdom (except Northern Ireland). See Appendix A.

14. Austria, Denmark, Greece, Norway, Sweden, and the United States; see Appendix B.

15. See Appendix A.

16. Law No. 75-17 of 17 January 1975, relating to the voluntary termination of pregnancy, Art. L. 162-1 (*J.O.* Jan. 18, 1975, p. 739), re-enacted and amended by Law No. 79-1204 of 31 December 1979, *J.O.* Jan. 1, 1980, p. 3. See Appendix C.

17. Ibid., Art. L. 162-4. If the pregnant woman is an unmarried minor, the consent of one of the persons who has parental authority over her, or of her legal representative, is required. Art. L. 162-7.

18. French Civil Code, Art. 212.

19. Ibid., Art. 213.

20. Law No. 75-17 of 17 January 1975, Art. 1.

21. Law No. 79-1204 of 31 December 1979, Art. 1.

22. Law No. 75-17 of 17 January 1975, Art. 13.

23. Ibid., Art. 1.

24. Ibid., Art. L. 162-1.

25. Law No. 79-1204 of 31 December 1979, Art. L. 162-3.

26. Ibid.

27. Ibid., Art. L. 162-4.

28. Ibid.

29. Ibid., Art. L. 162-5.

30. Ibid.

31. Ibid., Art. L. 162-12. One of the two must be chosen from an official list of approved experts.

32. Ibid., Art. L. 162-2 and L. 178-1.

33. French Code of Social Security, Art. L. 283, as amended by Law No. 82-1172, of 31 December 1982 (*Journal officiel* Jan. 1, 1983, p. 15).

34. The constitutional texts appealed to were the Preamble to the 1958 Constitution, which states that "every human being . . . possesses sacred and inalienable rights," and the Preamble to the 1946 Constitution, which states that the nation "guarantees protection of health to all, notably to children, and mothers." The law was also challenged on grounds that it violated the guarantee of the right to life in Article II of the European Convention on Human Rights, but the Constitutional Council declined to rule on this point. Jacques Robert, "La Décision du Conseil Constitutionnel du 15 janvier 1975 sur l'interruption volontaire de grossesse," 27 *Revue internationale de droit comparé* 873 (1975).

35. French Constitutional Council Decision of January 15, 1975 [1975] D.S. Jur. 529; *Journal officiel* Jan. 16, 1975, p. 671. For a discussion of constitutional review in France and a translation of the French abortion decision, see Mary Ann Glendon, Michael Wallace Gordon, and Christopher Osakwe, *Com-*

parative Legal Traditions: Text, Materials and Cases on the Civil Law, Common Law and Socialist Law Traditions (St. Paul: West Publishing Co., 1985), 72–82.

36. Montesquieu, *The Spirit of the Laws,* II, chap. 29.

37. See Robert, "La Décision du Conseil Constitutionnel."

38. See generally the articles in the special issue of the *Revue française de sociologie* devoted to the operation of the French abortion laws, 23-3 *Revue française de sociologie* (1982).

39. *City of Akron v. Akron Center for Reproductive Health, Inc.,* 462 U.S. 416 (1983).

40. 462 U.S. at 444.

41. Ibid.

42. *Thornburgh v. American College of Obstetricians and Gynecologists,* 54 U.S.L.W. 4618 (1986).

43. Ibid., at 4622.

44. Ibid., at 4622; *City of Akron v. Akron Center for Reproductive Health, Inc.,* 462 U.S. 416, 432–38 (1983); *Planned Parenthood Assn. v. Ashcroft,* 462 U.S. 476, 481–82 (1983).

45. *Roe v. Wade,* 410 U.S. 113, 165–66 (1973).

46. Lynn D. Wardle, "Rethinking Roe v. Wade," 1985 *Brigham Young University Law Review* 231, 244.

47. "For cause" countries which expressly permit abortion, at least in early pregnancy, if the mother's mental health would be endangered by the continuation of the pregnancy, are: France ("distress"), West Germany, Iceland, Italy, Luxembourg, the Netherlands ("distress"), Portugal, Spain, and the United Kingdom (except Northern Ireland). See Appendix A.

48. "For cause" countries which expressly permit abortion, at least in early pregnancy, if it is likely the child would be born with a serious defect are: France, West Germany, Iceland, Italy, Luxembourg, Portugal, Spain, and the United Kingdom (except Northern Ireland). See Appendix A.

49. "For cause" countries which expressly permit abortion, at least in early pregnancy, where the pregnancy results from a criminal act against the woman are: Finland, West Germany, Iceland, Italy ("circumstances under which conception occurred"), Luxembourg, Portugal, and Spain. See Appendix A.

50. "For cause" countries which expressly permit abortion, at least in early pregnancy, for various socioeconomic reasons are: Finland, France ("distress"), Iceland, and the Netherlands ("distress"). West Germany, Italy, Luxembourg, and the United Kingdom (except Northern Ireland) expressly permit such factors to be considered in evaluating the threat of pregnancy to the woman's health. See Appendix A.

51. The Italian abortion law of 1978 (*Gazzetta ufficiale,* Part 1, 22 May 1978, No. 140, 3642–46) begins with a declaration of the commitment of the state to "protect human life from its inception" and a statement that abortion is not to be a means of birth control (Art. 1). It then provides that women may request an abortion during the first ninety days if continuation of the pregnancy

"would seriously endanger their physical or mental health, in view of their state of health, their economic, social, or family circumstances, the circumstances in which conception occurred, or the probability that the child would be born with abnormalities or malformations" (Art. 4). As in France, a woman who has reached the age of majority is the judge of whether these circumstances exist. If she persists in her request, after mandatory counseling and information sessions and, except in emergency cases, following a seven-day period of "reflection," the abortion may be performed (Art. 5). As in the French statute, and in contrast to the Akron ordinance, the Italian provisions on information and counseling are designed to be nonthreatening to the pregnant woman. The phrase "with due respect for the dignity and personal feelings of the woman" is thrice repeated in these sections (Arts. 5 and 14). After ninety days abortions may be performed only where a physician certifies that the woman's physical or mental health or life is seriously in danger (Arts. 6 and 7). Where it is "possible" that the fetus may be viable, abortion may be performed only to save the life of the mother, and the physician must take "any appropriate action" to save the life of the fetus (Art. 7). An attempt to further liberalize this law and a proposal to reinstate strict control were both defeated in a popular referendum in 1981. See Christopher Tietze and Stanley K. Henshaw, *Induced Abortion: A World Review,* 6th ed. (New York: Guttmacher Institute, 1986), 22.

52. *Roe v. Wade,* 410 U.S. 113, 160 (1973).

53. *Roe v. Wade* held that states are permitted but not constitutionally required to pass legislation restricting abortion in the third trimester to protect the fetus, except where abortion "is necessary to preserve the life or health of the mother." Ibid., 164. According to Wardle and Wood, about half the states have elected to adopt legislation restricting abortions in the third trimester: Lynn Wardle and Mary Ann Wood, *A Lawyer Looks at Abortion* (Provo, Utah: Brigham Young University Press, 1982), 135.

54. 410 U.S. at 164.

55. 410 U.S. 179, 192 (1973).

56. *Colautti v. Franklin,* 439 U.S. 379 (1979); *Thornburgh v. American College of Obstetricians and Gynecologists,* 54 U.S.L.W. 4618 (1986). In *Planned Parenthood Assn. v. Ashcroft,* 462 U.S. 476 (1983), the Supreme Court upheld a Missouri statute requiring that a second physician be present at an abortion performed after viability, but it struck down a similar requirement in *Thornburgh* because it could find no implied exception in the Pennsylvania statute for emergency situations in which the mother's health might be endangered by delay in the arrival of a second physician. *Thornburgh v. American College of Obstetricians and Gynecologists,* 54 U.S.L.W. at 4624 (1986).

57. Austria: Federal Law of 23 January 1974, translated in 26 *International Digest of Health Legislation* 226 (1975). Denmark: Law No. 350 of 13 June 1973, translated in 24 *International Digest of Health Legislation* 773 (1973), as amended by Law No. 254 of 12 June 1975, translated in 27 *International Digest of Health Legislation* 113 (1976). Norway: Law No. 66 of 16 June

1978, translated in 30 *International Digest of Health Legislation* 126 (1979). See Appendix B. (The 1986 Greek statute has not yet been published in the *International Digest.*)

58. Swedish Abortion Law (No. 595) of 14 June 1974, translated in 25 *International Digest of Health Legislation* 618 (1974).

59. Ibid.

60. Ketting and van Praag, *Schwangerschaftsabbruch,* 13.

61. Swedish Abortion Law, Section 3.

62. Ibid., Sections 3 and 6.

63. The Swedish Institute, *Legislation on Family Planning* (Fact Sheets on Sweden, August 1982).

64. Ibid.

65. The birth rate among Swedish teenagers is less than half what it was in the 1970s (ibid.).

66. In East Germany abortion is available on the request of the pregnant woman during the first twelve weeks of pregnancy. After twelve weeks permission may be granted by a commission of medical specialists if continuation of the pregnancy would endanger the woman's life or for other serious reasons. Permission is to be granted to women who have terminated a pregnancy within the preceding six months only in exceptional cases. Law of 9 March 1972 on the interruption of pregnancy, 23 *International Digest of Health Legislation* 767 (1972). See also Penal Code of 12 January 1968, 24 *International Digest of Health Legislation* 157 (1973). A similar situation obtains in Czechoslovakia since 1986. (Jan Stepan's translation of the new Czech statutes will appear in the 1987 *International Digest.*) For the situation in the Soviet Union, see Christopher Osakwe, *Commentaries on the R.S.F.S.R. Criminal Code* (forthcoming).

67. In part, this movement has been in response to official concern about low birth rates. A countertrend seems to be beginning in Hungary.

In Bulgaria abortion on request is not permitted to childless women or women with one living child except in particularly serious circumstances, such as disease endangering woman's life or viability of offspring, rape or incest, unmarried women under eighteen with no living child or women over forty-five with one living child. Abortion may be prohibited if pregnancy exceeds ten weeks or if last abortion was less than six months ago or for medical contraindications. Every effort must be made to persuade women with two or fewer living children to continue pregnancy to term, but this is not required for women with three or more living children. Instruction No. 0-27 of the Ministry of Public Health to regulate the artificial interruption of pregnancy (D.V., 20 April 1973, No. 32, pp. 2–4), 24 *International Digest of Health Legislation* 730 (1973), as amended by D.V., 22 February 1974, No. 15, pp. 7–8, 25 *International Digest of Health Legislation* 541 (1974).

In Hungary abortion will be authorized by a committee only for specific reasons: medical problems (of woman or fetus); when the woman is single or separated and has been for six months; when pregnancy results from a criminal act; for lack of accommodations; when a woman has had at least three children or deliveries or when she is over thirty-five. Authorization may be granted to a woman who has two living children; when the health or viability of the fetus is threatened; if the woman or her spouse is serving a prison sentence of at least six months; or on other imperative social grounds. Resolution No. 1040 of 18 October 1973 and Ordinance No. 4 of 1 December 1973, 25 *International Digest of Health Legislation* 331 (1974). See also Law No. IV of 1978 on the Penal Code, 31 *International Digest of Health Legislation* 834 (1980), and Ordinance No. 3 of 10 February 1983, amending Ordinance No. 4, 33 *International Digest of Health Legislation* 494 (1982). A 1986 Ordinance effected some minor liberalizing changes in the Hungarian scheme of regulation, according to Jan Stepan of the Swiss Institute of Comparative Law.

In 1966 Romania made abortion available on request only to women who are over forty or under fourteen, or who have borne and are still caring for four or more children, or who are judged by a committee to be in danger of losing their lives, or who are pregnant by rape or incest, or incapacitated physically, psychologically or emotionally. Medical indications for termination are carefully specified. Further restrictions were added in 1984 and 1985. Decree No. 770 of 29 September 1966, 18 *International Digest of Health Legislation* 822 (1967). See also Decree No. 771 of 29 September 1966, 18 *International Digest of Health Legislation* 823 (1967), and Instructions No. 819 of 19 October 1966, 18 *International Digest of Health Legislation* 824 (1967), and revisions, 25 *International Digest of Health Legislation* 433 (1974) and 27 *International Digest of Health Legislation* 803 (1976). C. Tietze and S. Henshaw, *Induced Abortion*, 23.

68. *Thornburgh v. American College of Obstetricians and Gynecologists*, 54 U.S.L.W. 4618, 4628 (1986) (Burger, C.J., dissenting).

69. United Nations Fund for Population Activities, *Annual Review of Population Law, 1979* (1980), 21.

70. United Nations Fund for Population Activities, *Annual Review of Population Law, 1981* (1982), 15. C. Tietze and S. Henshaw, *Induced Abortion*, 25.

71. *Bellotti v. Baird* (Bellotti I), 428 U.S. 132 (1976); *Bellotti v. Baird* (Bellotti II), 443 U.S. 622, 639 (1979).

72. *City of Akron v. Akron Center for Reproductive Health Inc.*, 462 U.S. 416, 419 n. 1 (1983).

73. *Roe v. Wade*, 410 U.S. 113 (1973) (no regulation of first trimester abortions, regulation in the second trimester only to protect the health of the pregnant woman, and regulation in the interest of the fetus permitted but not required only after viability, subject to the requirement that abortions be permitted to preserve the life or health of the pregnant woman). See also, especially, *Doe v. Bolton*, 410 U.S. 179 (1973) (requirement of two-doctor concurrence with physician's judgment and advance approval by a hospital abortion committee for abortions at any stage of pregnancy unconstitutional); *Planned Parenthood of Central Missouri v. Danforth*, 428 U.S. 52 (1976) (spousal and parental consent requirements held unconstitutional); *Colautti v. Franklin*, 439 U.S.

379 (1979) (various limitations on a doctor's choice of abortion techniques so as to provide the best opportunity for the fetus to be born alive held unconstitutional); *City of Akron v. Akron Center for Reproductive Health Inc.,* 462 U.S. 416 (1983) (holding unconstitutional a city ordinance requiring physician to inform pregnant woman, before her consent to abortion, of state of development of fetus, risks of abortion, and availability of assistance from agencies, and imposing a twenty-four-hour waiting period after consent); *Thornburgh v. American College of Obstetricians and Gynecologists,* 54 U.S.L.W. 4618 (1986) (mandatory information about risks of abortion, possible availability of medical assistance and child support, and availability of printed matter concerning characteristics of fetus and organizations to assist with alternatives to abortion held unconstitutional; provisions regulating postviability abortions also struck down).

74. Mauro Cappelletti and William Cohen, *Comparative Constitutional Law* (Indianapolis: Bobbs-Merrill, 1979), 563–622, contains translations of edited constitutional abortion decisions from Austria, France, West Germany and Italy. The 1985 Spanish decision, which substantially upheld Spain's abortion law, is discussed in Richard Stith, "Constitutional and Penal Perspectives on Spanish Abortion Law," *American Journal of Comparative Law* (forthcoming, Summer 1987).

75. Judgment of Feb. 25, 1975, 39 BVerfG E 1. English translations: *The Abortion Decision of February 25, 1975, of the Federal Constitutional Court, Federal Republic of Germany,* Edmund C. Jann trans. (Washington, D.C.: Library of Congress, 1975) (hereafter Jann); "West German Abortion Decision: A Contrast to *Roe v. Wade,*" Robert E. Jonas and John D. Gorby, trans., 9 *John Marshall Journal of Practice and Procedure* 605 (1976) (hereafter Jonas and Gorby).

76. Fifth Statute to Reform the Penal Law of June 18, 1974 (Bundesgesetzblatt I, 1297). The statute is translated in Jann.

77. Under *Roe v. Wade* a state may regulate abortion subsequent to the first trimester and prior to viability only "in ways that are reasonably related to maternal health." 410 U.S. at 164.

78. The procedure of "abstract" judicial review through which a federal or state government or a third of the members of the Bundestag may request review of a statute's constitutionality without a specific case or controversy is described in Ernst Benda, "Constitutional Jurisdiction in West Germany," 19 *Columbia Journal of Transnational Law* 1 (1981).

79. Basic Law of the Federal Republic of Germany, Art. 2(2): "Everyone shall have the right to life and to inviolability of his person. The liberty of the individual shall be inviolable. These rights may only be encroached upon pursuant to a law." Art. 1(1): "The dignity of man shall be inviolable. To respect and protect it shall be the duty of all state authority." *The Basic Law of the Federal Republic of Germany* (West German Press and Information Office, 1981), 14.

80. Jann, 27, 50–51. Since the statute under review forbade abortions only after the fourteenth day from conception, the court's decision was that "devel-

oping life" is present at least from that time onward. The fourteen-day period relates to the approximate time of implantation of the fertilized ovum in the uterus and to individuation of development.

81. Ibid., 6, 91.

82. Ibid., 50, 57, 58–59.

83. Ibid.

84. Ibid.

85. Ibid., 50–51.

86. In addition to the rights to life and liberty already quoted, Art. 2 of the Basic Law guarantees that "(1) Everyone shall have the right to free development of his personality insofar as he does not violate the rights of others or offend against the constitutional order or the moral code." *Basic Law of the Federal Republic of Germany* (West German Press and Information Office, 1981), 14.

87. Jann, 56, 57, 63–64.

88. Ibid., 60, 62–63.

89. Ibid., 70. Under the pre-1974 law all abortion was stated to be criminal, but a landmark decision in 1927 had admitted the defense of necessity where continuation of the pregnancy posed a grave danger to the life or health of the pregnant woman. Reichsgericht Decision of March 11, 1927 (61 RGSt. 242).

90. Ibid., 61.

91. Ibid., 63.

92. Ibid., 64.

93. Ibid., 71.

94. Ibid., 67.

95. Ibid., 58, 65–66.

96. Ibid., 66–67.

97. Ibid., 67, 68.

98. Ibid., 67–68.

99. Ibid., 60.

100. Ibid.

101. Ibid., 63, 68.

102. Ibid., 72, 82–87.

103. Ibid., 7.

104. Ibid.

105. Jonas and Gorby, 654–55.

106. *Roe v. Wade,* 410 U.S. 113, 116 (1973).

107. Jann, 89.

108. Jonas and Gorby, 662.

109. Ibid., 667.

110. West German Constitutional Court Decision, Jann, 96–97.

111. Ibid.

112. Ibid., 93.

113. Ibid., 130.

114. Ibid., 129.

115. Ibid., 131.

116. Fifteenth Statute to Reform the Penal Law of May 18, 1976 (Bundesgesetzblatt I, 1213), translated in *Annual Review of Population Law, 1976* (1977), 49.

117. Ibid., Sections 218, 218a.

118. Ibid., Section 218b.

119. Ibid.

120. Ibid., Section 218.

121. *Brüggemann and Scheuten v. Federal Republic of Germany,* 3 E.H.R.R. 244 (1977).

122. Ibid., 251.

123. Ibid., 253, 254.

124. Ibid., 254–55.

125. Eike von Hippel, "Besserer Schutz des Embryos vor Abtreibung?" *Juristenzeitung* 53, 56 (1986).

126. Winfried Kluth, "Zur Rechtsnatur der indizierten Abtreibung," *Zeitschrift für das gesamte Familienrecht* 440 (1985).

127. Aristotle, *Nicomachean Ethics* 3.1.1000a.

128. Von Hippel, "Besserer Schutz," 55.

129. Such regulations are, however, authorized by the Law on the Federal Constitutional Court of March 12, 1951 (translated in Jann, 124–25), which provides that the court may "temporarily regulate a situation by way of a provisional order" if there are urgent reasons for doing so.

130. "We need not resolve the difficult question of when life begins." *Roe v. Wade,* 410 U.S. 113, 159 (1973). "The word 'person,' as used in the Fourteenth Amendment, does not include the unborn." 410 U.S. at 158.

131. For example, *Dred Scott v. Sandford,* 60 U.S. 393, 404–05 (1857); *Commonwealth v. Welosky,* 276 Mass. 398 (1931).

132. 405 U.S. 438 (1972).

133. J. Noonan, *A Private Choice,* 21.

134. Donald Kommers, "Abortion and the Constitution: The Cases of the United States and West Germany," in *Abortion: New Directions for Policy Studies,* ed. Edward Manier, William Liu, and David Solomon (Notre Dame, Ind.: University of Notre Dame Press, 1977), 83, 107–09; D. Kommers, "Liberty and Community in Constitutional Law: The Abortion Cases in Comparative Perspective," 1985 *Brigham Young University Law Review* 371, 399–409.

135. Douglas, J., concurring opinion in *Roe v. Wade, Doe v. Bolton,* 410 U.S. 113, 214 (1973): "The clear message of these cases—[is] that a woman is free to make the basic decision whether to bear an unwanted child. Elaborate argument is hardly necessary to demonstrate that childbirth may deprive a woman of her preferred lifestyle and force upon her a radically different and undesired future."

136. Laurence Tribe, "Structural Due Process," 10 *Harvard Civil Rights-Civil Liberties Law Review* 269, 321 (1975).

137. Archibald Cox, *The Role of the Supreme Court in American Government* (New York: Oxford University Press, 1976), 114.

138. See Michael Sandel, "Morality and the Liberal Ideal," *The New Republic*, 7 May 1984, 15.

139. Samuel Warren and Louis Brandeis, "The Right to Privacy," 4 *Harvard Law Review* 193 (1890).

140. Ibid., 193. See also *Olmstead v. United States*, 277 U.S. 438, 478 (1928) (Brandeis, J., dissenting).

141. 381 U.S. 479 (1965).

142. 405 U.S. 438, 453 (1972).

143. 410 U.S. 113 (1973).

144. Basil S. Markesinis, "Conceptualism, Pragmatism and Courage: A Common Lawyer Looks at Some Judgments of the German Federal Court," 34 *American Journal of Comparative Law* 349, 359 (1986).

145. Leo Strauss, *Natural Right and History* (Chicago: University of Chicago Press, 1953), 294.

146. Quoted in Markesinis, "Conceptualism, Pragmatism and Courage," 360–61.

147. *Bowers v. Hardwick*, 106 S. Ct. 2841 (1986).

148. Stith, "Constitutional and Penal Perspectives."

149. K. Luker, *Abortion and the Politics of Motherhood*, 2.

150. Robert Bellah, Richard Madsen, William Sullivan, Ann Swidler and Stephen Tipton, *Habits of the Heart: Individualism and Commitment in American Life* (Berkeley: University of California Press, 1985).

151. Gilbert Y. Steiner, *The Futility of Family Policy* (Washington, D.C.: Brookings Institution, 1981), 71. "Neither constitutional change nor additional legislation concerning abortion is politically feasible, not because either side lacks the necessary intensity of feeling to make the required effort, but exactly because the issue is so divisive that politicians shy away from the consequences of winning" (ibid., 58–59).

152. Brigitte Berger and Peter Berger, *The War over the Family: Capturing the Middle Ground* (New York: Anchor Books, 1983), 81.

153. Judith Blake, "The Supreme Court's Abortion Decisions and Public Opinion in the United States," 27 September 1978, *Congressional Record*, 95th Cong., 2d sess., S. 31910, 31911; Mary Ann Lamanna, "Social Science and Ethical Issues: The Policy Implications of Poll Data on Abortion," in *Abortion: Understanding Differences*, ed. Sidney Callahan and Daniel Callahan (New York and London: Plenum Press, 1984), 1, 3.

154. Ibid.; Judith Blake, "The Abortion Decisions: Judicial Review and Public Opinion," in *Abortion: New Directions for Policy Studies*, ed. Edward Manier, William Liu, and David Solomon (Notre Dame, Ind.: University of Notre Dame Press, 1977), 51, 80. J. Blake, "Abortion and Public Opinion: The 1960–1970 Decade," 171 *Science* 540 (1971).

155. A 1985 Gallup survey showed 22 percent in favor of abortions on

demand, 57 percent in favor of abortions under certain circumstances, and 22 percent in favor of a total ban except where the pregnant woman's life is in danger. This basic pattern has changed very little since 1975. Digest, 17 *Family Planning Perspectives* 76 (1985).

156. Donald Granberg and Beth W. Granberg, "Abortion Attitudes, 1965–1980: Trends and Determinants," 12 *Family Planning Perspectives* 250, 252 (1980). J. Blake, "Supreme Court's Abortion Decisions," 31913. J. Blake, "The Abortion Decisions," 80.

157. J. Blake, "Supreme Court's Abortion Decisions," 31913.

158. Ibid.

159. Ibid., 31912.

160. John E. Jackson and Maris A. Vinovskis, "Public Opinion, Elections and the 'Single-Issue' Issue," in *The Abortion Dispute and the American System*, ed. Gilbert Steiner (Washington, D.C.: Brookings Institution, 1983), 64. See also, Judith Blake and Jorge H. Del Pinal, "Negativism, Equivocation, and Wobbly Assent: Public 'Support' for the Pro-choice Platform on Abortion," 18 *Demography* 309 (1981).

161. Jackson and Vinovskis, "Public Opinion," 65.

162. Sidney Callahan and Daniel Callahan, "Breaking Through the Stereotypes," *Commonweal,* 5 October 1984, 520, 523.

163. Daniel Degnan, "Law, Morals and Abortion," *Commonweal,* 31 May 1974, 305, 306–07.

164. Such an amendment has been drafted by John Noonan. See J. Noonan, *A Private Choice,* 185–88.

165. *City of Akron v. Akron Center for Reproductive Health, Inc.,* 462 U.S. 416, 419–420 (1983); *Thornburgh v. American College of Obstetricians and Gynecologists,* 42 U.S.L.W. 4618 (1986).

166. *Planned Parenthood of Missouri v. Danforth,* 428 U.S. 53, 92 (1976); *Colautti v. Franklin,* 439 U.S. 379, 401 (1979); *Thornburgh v. American College of Obstetricians and Gynecologists,* 42 U.S.L.W. 4618, 4627 (1986).

167. *Roe v. Wade,* 410 U.S. 113, 118 (1973).

168. "Carmosina et al., Decision of the Italian Constitutional Court of February 18, 1975," translated in Mauro Cappelletti and William Cohen, *Comparative Constitutional Law* (Indianapolis: Bobbs-Merrill, 1979), 612–14.

169. See n. 51 above.

170. *City of Akron v. Akron Center for Reproductive Health, Inc.,* 462 U.S. 416, 459 (1983). (Emphasis in original).

171. Ibid., 461.

172. Ibid., 465.

173. Ibid., 458.

174. Ibid.

175. Archibald Cox, *The Role of the Supreme Court in American Government* (New York: Oxford University Press, 1976), 53–55, 114; Alexander M. Bickel, *The Morality of Consent* (New Haven: Yale University Press, 1975), 28:

"Should not the question . . . have been left to the political process, which in state after state can achieve not one but many accommodations, adjusting them from time to time as attitudes change?"; John Hart Ely, "The Wages of Crying Wolf: A Comment on *Roe v. Wade*," 82 *Yale Law Journal* 920 (1973); Harry H. Wellington, "Common Law Rules and Constitutional Double Standards: Some Notes on Adjudication," 83 *Yale Law Journal* 223, 297 ff. (1973); Richard Epstein, "Substantive Due Process by Any Other Name: The Abortion Cases," 1973 *Supreme Court Review* 159; Paul A. Freund, "Storms over the Supreme Court," 69 *American Bar Association Journal* 1474, 1480 (1983).

176. Compare Laurence Tribe, "The Supreme Court, 1972 Term—Foreword: Toward a Model of Roles in the Due Process of Life and Law," 87 *Harvard Law Review* 1, 21–25 (1973), with Laurence Tribe, *American Constitutional Law* (Mineola, N.Y.: Foundation Press, 1978), 928.

177. See generally, Michael Perry, *The Constitution, the Courts and Human Rights: An Inquiry into the Legitimacy of Constitutional Policymaking by the Judiciary* (New Haven: Yale University Press, 1982); Laurence Tribe, "Structural Due Process," 10 *Harvard Civil Rights-Civil Liberties Law Review* 269, 321 (1975); Laurence Tribe, *American Constitutional Law,* 11–13.

178. It seems that the best way for the Supreme Court to fulfill the role Tribe and Perry would like it to play would be for it to set forth its views in essays, rather than stating them in such a way as to preclude future political action.

179. Michael Perry, "Abortion, the Public Morals, and the Police Power: The Ethical Function of Substantive Due Process," 23 *U.C.L.A. Law Review* 689, 733 (1976).

180. Ibid., 733.

181. Ibid., n. 204. The poll showed that one-third supported a more permissive approach than the court had taken, one-third favored a more restrictive approach, and one-third favored the *Roe* result.

182. Michael Perry, "The Authority of Text, Tradition, and Reason: A Theory of Constitutional 'Interpretation,' " 58 *Southern California Law Review* 551, 559 n. 27 (1985); Michael Perry, "Substantive Due Process Revisited: Reflections on (and Beyond) Recent Cases," 71 *Northwestern University Law Review* 417, 468 (1976).

183. Ibid.

184. Ibid.

185. D. Degnan, "Law, Morals and Abortion," 305, 306.

186. Aristotle, *Nicomachean Ethics,* Book 5.

187. Guido Calabresi, *Ideals, Beliefs, Attitudes, and the Law* (New York: Syracuse University Press, 1985), 97.

188. Ibid.

189. K. Luker, *Abortion and the Politics of Motherhood,* 158–91.

190. G. Calabresi, *Ideals, Beliefs, Attitudes,* 109.

191. Survey of Abortion Law, 1980 *Arizona State Law Journal* 67, 109–111.

192. *Roe v. Wade*, 410 U.S. 113, 117–18 (1973).

193. J. Noonan, *A Private Choice*, 33.

194. Max Rheinstein, *Marriage Stability, Divorce, and the Law* (Chicago: University of Chicago Press, 1972), 55–105.

195. See "1985 Survey of American Family Law," 11 *Family Law Reporter* (BNA) 3015 (1985).

196. See the summaries of the various state laws in *Family Law Reporter* (BNA), Reference File, State Divorce Laws 401:001–451:001.

197. American Law Institute, Model Penal Code, Section 230.3 (Proposed Official Draft, 1962) would have made abortion a crime unless two physicians certified they believed the abortion justified because the pregnancy would gravely impair the physical or mental health of the woman, the child would be born with a serious mental or physical defect, or the pregnancy resulted from rape, incest, or other felonious act. The section is set forth in full in *Doe v. Bolton*, 410 U.S. 179, 205 (1973).

198. National Conference of Commissioners on Uniform State Laws, Uniform Abortion Act of 1972. This act would have permitted abortion in early pregnancy, if the continuation of the pregnancy was likely to endanger the life or gravely impair the physical or mental health of the mother, or if it was likely that the child would be born with a grave mental or physical defect, or if the pregnancy resulted from rape, incest, or illicit intercourse with a girl under the age of 16. The act is set forth in *Roe v. Wade*, 410 U.S. 113, 146 n. 40 (1973).

199. See "Survey of Abortion Law," *Arizona State Law Journal*, 106–112.

200. *Roe v. Wade*, 410 U.S. 113, 139–140 (1973).

201. 410 U.S. at 720 n. 37.

202. Ketting and van Praag, *Schwangerschaftsabbruch*, 88.

203. Walter Sullivan, "Scientists Developing a New Drug That Blocks and Halts Pregnancy," *New York Times*, October 13, 1986, p. A15.

204. Ruth Bader Ginsburg, "Some Thoughts on Autonomy and Equality in Relation to *Roe v. Wade*," 63 *North Carolina Law Review* 375 (1985); Laurence Tribe, *Constitutional Choices* (Cambridge, Mass.: Harvard University Press, 1985), 59.

205. The extensive judicial deference in the abortion cases to the discretion of doctors has been noted and criticized in Andrea Asaro, "The Judicial Portrayal of the Physician in Abortion and Sterilization Decisions: The Use and Abuse of Medical Discretion," 6 *Harvard Women's Law Journal* 51 (1983), and Charles H. Baron, " 'If You Prick Us, Do We Not Bleed?': Of Shylock, Fetuses, and the Concept of Person in the Law," 11 *Law, Medicine and Health Care* 52 (1983).

206. The best exposition of this point I have seen was made by Katha Pollitt, who has suggested that noncelibate men who oppose abortion, rather than directing their moral fervor against women, should exhort their fellows never to sleep with a woman unless prepared to marry her if she becomes pregnant; to support every child they father until that child is twenty-one; to share fully in child care

even if that means sacrificing some job opportunities; and to take responsibility for birth control. Katha Pollitt, "Hentoff, Are You Listening?" *Mother Jones* February-March 1985, 60.

207. Carol Gilligan, *In a Different Voice: Psychological Theory and Women's Development* (Cambridge, Mass.: Harvard University Press, 1982), 5.

208. Ibid., 73.

209. Gail Pool, "Women's Different Voice: The Ethic of Care," *Radcliffe Quarterly,* September 1982, 6, 7.

210. Ibid.

211. Ibid., 8.

212. Gilligan, *In a Different Voice,* 171, 173.

213. Kenneth L. Karst, "Woman's Constitution," 1984 *Duke Law Journal* 447.

214. Ibid., 461, 475.

215. Jann, 131.

216. Blake, "Abortion and Public Opinion," 544.

217. Ibid.

218. Catharine MacKinnon, "*Roe v. Wade:* A Study in Male Ideology," in *Abortion: Moral and Legal Perspectives,* ed. Jay L. Garfield (Amherst: University of Massachusetts Press, 1984), 45, 53.

219. Gilligan, *In a Different Voice,* 81, 88, 89, 91.

220. Sheila B. Kamerman and Alfred J. Kahn, eds., *Family Policy: Government and Families in Fourteen Countries* (New York: Columbia University Press, 1978); Sheila B. Kamerman and Alfred J. Kahn, *Child Care, Family Benefits, and Working Parents: A Study in Comparative Policy* (New York: Columbia University Press, 1981), 211, 237, 241, 248; Alfred J. Kahn and Sheila B. Kamerman, *Income Transfers for Families with Children: An Eight Country Study* (Philadelphia: Temple University Press, 1983), 157, 182–83, 307; Sheila B. Kamerman, Alfred J. Kahn, and Paul Kingston, *Maternity Policies and Working Women* (New York: Columbia University Press, 1983).

For a survey of the various ways in which the member nations of the European Communities assist working mothers and pregnant women, see Dagmar Coester-Waltjen, *Mutterschutz in Europa* (Munich: Schweitzer, 1986).

221. Sheila B. Kamerman, "Child-Care Services: A National Picture," 106 *Monthly Labor Review* 35, 39 (1983).

222. Sheila B. Kamerman and Alfred J. Kahn, "The Day-Care Debate: A Wider View," 54 *The Public Interest* 78, 90 (1979).

223. Ibid.

224. Ibid.

225. Ibid., 91.

226. Ibid., 92.

227. S. Kamerman and A. Kahn, *Child Care, Family Benefits, and Working Parents,* 229–36.

228. Ibid., 248.

229. *Harris v. McRae,* 448 U.S. 297 (1980), upholding the "Hyde Amendment" to Title XIX of the Social Security Act, excluding abortions from Medicaid coverage; and *Maher v. Roe,* 432 U.S. 464 (1977); *Poelker v. Doe,* 432 U.S. 519 (1977), and *Beal v. Doe,* 432 U.S. 438 (1977), all upholding state denial of medical expenses or hospital facilities for nontherapeutic abortions sought by indigent women.

230. S. Kamerman and A. Kahn, *Child Care, Family Benefits and Working Parents,* 207, 212–13.

231. U.S. Dept. of Commerce, Bureau of the Census, *Characteristics of the Population Below the Poverty Level,* Table 11, 1983 Consumer Income Series P-60, No. 147.

232. As of January 1985, fifteen jurisdictions continued to pay for abortions with state Medicaid funds: Alaska, California, Connecticut, District of Columbia, Hawaii, Maryland, Massachusetts, Michigan, New Jersey, New York, North Carolina, Oregon, Washington, West Virginia, and Vermont. Ten of these did so pursuant to statute; five pursuant to state court decisions. (Alan Guttmacher Institute, information compiled by Robyn Smith and Rachel Benson Gold, January 1985.) Twelve of these fifteen are among the top twenty jurisdictions with the highest per capita public aid expenditures. Three of these, California, New York and Michigan, accounted for 34 percent of all Medicaid eligible people in 1983. (Bureau of the Census, *Statistical Abstract of the United States* 1985, 105th ed., 1984, 278, 373, 380.)

233. C. Geertz, *Local Knowledge: Further Essays in Interpretive Anthropology* (New York: Basic Books, 1983), 217.

234. *Doe v. Bolton,* 410 U.S. 179, 192 (1973). (Doctor's medical judgment relating to health of pregnant women "may be exercised in the light of all factors—physical, emotional, psychological, familial, and the woman's age—relevant to the well-being of the patient.")

235. C. Tietze and S. Henshaw, *Induced Abortion,* 29, Table 2.

236. Ibid.

237. M. Rheinstein, *Marriage Stability, Divorce and the Law.*

238. In 1984 the abortion rate in Italy was 19.0 per thousand women of child-bearing age, as compared to 12.8 for England and Wales, 10.2 for Canada, and 7.3 for the Federal Republic. Tietze and Henshaw, *Induced Abortion,* Table 2.

239. *Newsweek,* 14 January 1985, 26.

240. I am grateful to the distinguished Boston College theologian Ernest L. Fortin for acquainting me with this aspect of Poirot's thought.

241. Jonathan Glover, "Matters of Life and Death," *The New York Review of Books,* 30 May 1985, 19, 20.

242. Robert A. Burt, "Authorizing Death for Anomalous Newborns," in *Genetics and the Law,* ed. Aubrey Milunsky and George J. Annas (New York: Plenum Press, 1976), 435, 436. (*Roe v. Wade* "dramatically changed the context of current debate" and has had "significant generative impact" on issues related to newborns.)

243. See J. Noonan, *A Private Choice*, 63, 190.

244. C. Geertz, *Local Knowledge*, 234.

2. Divorce Law

1. Mary Ann Glendon, *State, Law, and Family: Family Law in Transition in the United States and Western Europe* (Amsterdam: North Holland Publishing Co., 1977).

2. Ibid.; Mary Ann Glendon, *The New Family and the New Property* (Toronto: Butterworths, 1981).

3. Representative of the American literature on this subject are: Walter Wadlington, "Divorce without Fault without Perjury," 52 *Virginia Law Review* 32 (1966); and Harvey Couch, "Toward a More Realistic Divorce Law," 43 *Tulane Law Review* 243 (1969).

4. Max Rheinstein, *Marriage Stability, Divorce, and the Law* (Chicago: University of Chicago Press, 1972), 258.

5. *Putting Asunder: A Divorce Law for Contemporary Society, The Report of a Group Appointed by the Archbishop of Canterbury in January 1964* (London: S.P.C.K., 1966); The Law Commission, *Reform of the Grounds of Divorce: The Field of Choice* (Command Paper 3123) (London: H.M.S.O., 1966).

6. The Law Commission, *Reform of the Grounds of Divorce*, par. 15.

7. *Putting Asunder*, 38.

8. Summaries of West European divorce laws can be found in A. Bergmann and Murad Ferid, *Internationales Ehe-und Kindschaftsrecht* (Frankfurt: Verlag für Standesamtswesen), a multivolume treatise kept current with loose-leaf supplements; and in J. Commaille et al., *Le Divorce en Europe occidentale: La Loi et le nombre* (Paris: I.N.E.D., 1983). For comparative treatments of divorce laws in selected countries, see M. Glendon, *State, Law, and Family;* J. Pousson-Petit, *Le Démariage en droit comparé* (Brussels: F. Larcier, 1981); and M. Rheinstein, *Marriage Stability*. The divorce laws of the American states are summarized and kept up to date in Family Law Reporter (BNA), Reference File, State Divorce Laws (with loose-leaf supplements).

9. In the Netherlands a divorce sought by one spouse alone can be denied if the other spouse is opposed and the plaintiff is found to have been primarily responsible for the breakdown of the marriage: Netherlands *Civil Code*, Art. 152. In West Germany spouses who have lived apart for less than a year can be divorced only if "continuation of the marriage would present an insupportable hardship for the petitioner" for reasons which are personally attributable to the other spouse: West German *Bürgerliches Gesetzbuch* Section 1565(2).

10. Netherlands *Civil Code*, Art. 152. In West Germany a divorce can be denied if the continuation of the marriage appears "exceptionally necessary" in the interests of minor children, or if divorce "by reason of extraordinary circum-

stances" would pose "severe hardship" for the nonconsenting spouse: West German *Bürgerliches Gesetzbuch* Section 1568(1).

11. West German *Bürgerliches Gesetzbuch* Section 1566(2).

12. The rarely used power of the courts in a handful of states to deny a unilateral no-fault divorce if a reasonable prospect of reconciliation exists is not a brake on unilateral divorce, but merely addressed to hasty divorce.

13. The Divorce Reform Act of 1969 went into effect in 1971. It is now consolidated in the Matrimonial Causes Act 1973, as amended by the Matrimonial and Family Proceedings Act 1984.

14. Matrimonial Causes Act 1973, Section 5.

15. In addition to the rather remote possibility of denial under the hardship clause, a divorce sought on the grounds of two years' separation with consent or five years' separation without consent may be delayed because of the court's power to refuse to make the decree absolute until it is satisfied that the financial provision, if any, to be made for the respondent is reasonable and fair, or the best that can be made under the circumstances. Ibid., Section 10(2)–10(4). In divorces involving couples with minor children, the judge is not to grant the decree until he finds that the parties' arrangements for their children's future are "satisfactory or the best that can be devised in the circumstances." Ibid., Section 41. These judicial powers of review have been reduced to a rubber-stamping of the couples' agreement in most cases.

16. Susan Maidment, "Family Law Practitioner," *New Law Journal,* 18 October 1985, 1028.

17. The Matrimonial and Family Proceedings Act 1984.

18. Brenda Hoggett and David Pearl, *The Family, Law and Society* (London: Butterworths, 1983), 179.

19. The French statute is described in detail in Glendon, *State, Law, and Family,* 202–14.

20. In 1984, 51 percent of all divorces in France were on fault grounds; 48 percent were granted under the mutual consent procedure; and one percent were on the ground of "prolonged disruption of the life in common." 4 *Statistique annuelle: Les Procès civils* (Paris, Ministère de la Justice, 1986), Table D1.

21. Jean Carbonnier, *Essais sur les lois* (Paris: Defrénois, 1979), 125–26.

22. Ibid., 129.

23. *Code Civil,* Arts. 237, 238.

24. Ibid., Art. 240.

25. Olivier Guillod, "La Clause de dureté dans quelques législations européens sur le divorce," *Revue internationale de droit comparé* 787, 808 (1983).

26. Ibid.

27. Court of Cassation 18 April 1980, 11 *Bulletin Civil* No. 73; Court of Cassation 28 April 1980, 11 *Bulletin Civil* No. 90.

28. *Recueil Dalloz* J. 520 (1984).

29. Guillod, "La Clause de dureté."

30. Ibid., 801. See also Claude Colombet et al., *Dictionnaire juridique: Divorce* (Paris: Dalloz, 1984), 82.

31. The prior as well as the 1976 German law is described in Glendon, *State, Law, and Family*, 217–22.

32. *Bürgerliches Gesetzbuch*, Sections 1565, 1566.

33. Ibid., Section 1565(2).

34. Ibid., Section 1568(1).

35. Decision of the Bundesverfassungsgericht, reported in *Neue Juristiche Wochenschrift* 108 (1981).

36. Guillod, "La Clause de dureté," 808.

37. The Swedish legislation is described in Glendon, *State, Law, and Family*, 222–27.

38. Quoted in Jacob Sundberg, "Recent Changes in Swedish Family Law: Experiment Repeated," 23 *American Journal of Comparative Law* 34, 44 (1975).

39. Note, "Sweden—Family Law," 22 *International and Comparative Law Quarterly* 182, 183 (1973).

40. See the Netherlands Civil Code, Section 152. Several state divorce laws do permit the court (where it has jurisdiction to do so) to make the divorce decree conditional on the spouses having made satisfactory arrangements for child custody and support, spousal maintenance, and property division.

41. The Mississippi and New York statutes do not permit no-fault divorce where one spouse is opposed. Miss. Code Ann. Section 93-5-2 (1985); N.Y. Dom. Rel. Law Section 170 (McKinney, 1985).

42. Herma H. Kay, "Making Marriage and Divorce Safe for Women" (book review), 60 *California Law Review* 1683, 1686 (1972).

43. Reprinted in Judith Areen, *Cases and Materials on Family Law*, 2d ed. (Mineola, N.Y.: Foundation Press, 1985), 268.

44. Uniform Marriage and Divorce Act Section 305, Comment.

45. Ibid., Section 302, Comment.

46. 401 U.S. 371 (1971). (Connecticut statute requiring payment of court fees and costs to obtain divorce held unconstitutional insofar as it operated to deny indigent persons access to judicial termination of marriage.)

47. 434 U.S. 374 (1978). (Wisconsin statute prohibiting marriage by any resident obligated to support minor children not in his custody, unless he could demonstrate to a court that his support obligations had been met and the children were not likely to become public charges, held to violate Equal Protection Clause of the Fourteenth Amendment.)

48. Areen, *Cases and Materials*, 272. The same understanding of breakdown grounds is found in *Putting Asunder*, 23–24.

49. Telephone conversation between Jeffrey O'Connell and the author, February 13, 1986.

50. Rheinstein, *Marriage Stability*, 368.

51. Areen, *Cases and Materials*, 272.

52. See, generally, for comparative treatments of postdivorce support and property issues: *Unterhaltsrecht in Europa*, ed. Peter Doppfel and Bernd Buchhofer (Tübingen: Mohr, 1983), a study of support law in twelve countries; Max Rheinstein and Mary Ann Glendon, "Marriage: Interspousal Relations," *International Encyclopedia of Comparative Law* (Tübingen: Mohr, 1980), IV, chap. 4, a worldwide survey of marital property law; and chap. 6 of Glendon, *State, Law, and Family*, which treats the economic consequences of divorce in England, France, Sweden, West Germany, and the United States. For recent trends in marital property law, see Jacques Grossen, "Comparative Developments in the Law of Matrimonial Regimes," 60 *Tulane Law Review* 1199 (1986).

53. *Putting Asunder*, 48.

54. M.-T. Meulders-Klein, "Financial Agreements on Divorce and the Freedom of Contract in Continental Europe," in *The Resolution of Family Conflict: Comparative Legal Perspectives*, ed. John Eekelaar and Sanford N. Katz (Toronto: Butterworths, 1984), 297.

55. *Bürgerliches Gesetzbuch*, former Section 1579.

56. Ibid., as amended in 1986.

57. See generally Catherine Labrusse-Riou, "Securité d'existence et solidarité familiale en droit privé: Etude comparative du droit des pays européens continentaux," *Revue internationale de droit comparé* 829–65 (1986).

58. For example, F. W. Bosch, "Ruckblick und Ausblick," *Zeitschrift für das gesamte Familienrecht* 739, 746 (1980): "The consequences of marriage dissolution are now more onerous than before"; Wolfram Müller-Freienfels, "Review Essay," 33 *American Journal of Comparative Law* 733, 744 (1985): "[The German legislature] has made divorce more economically difficult, even economically impossible"; Michelle Gobert, "Aperçu de la loi française sur le divorce du 11 juillet 1975," *Bulletin de l'institut international de droit d'expression française* 12 (1975).

59. French Civil Code, Art. 270.

60. Ibid.

61. Ibid., Art. 278.

62. Ibid., Art. 280–1.

63. Ibid., Art. 281.

64. See Anders Agell, "Social Security and Family Law in Sweden," in *Social Security and Family Law with Special Reference to the One-Parent Family: A Comparative Survey*, ed. Alec Samuels (London: United Kingdom Comparative Law Series, 1979), IV, 149, 158–60.

65. See ibid. for a description of the collection system. The relative generosity of the Swedish benefit-service package is described in S. Kamerman and A. Kahn, *Income Transfers for Families with Children: An Eight-Country Study*, (Philadelphia: Temple University Press, 1983), 60, 71.

66. In most of continental Europe, and in three of the eight American community property states (California, Louisiana and New Mexico), marital property (usually defined to include all the property acquired by either spouse

during the marriage except by gift or inheritance) is in principle divided equally. England and the overwhelming majority of the American states, however, have replaced the old "his" and "hers" separate property system or (in five community property states) the traditional community property rule of 50–50 division with judicial discretion to reallocate the spouses' property after divorce in the way that seems to the judge "fair" or "equitable."

67. Numerous studies in England and the United States document that custodial parents, usually mothers, bear the main economic responsibility for children after divorce, and that the standard of living of the custodial parent's household typically declines after divorce, while that of the noncustodial parent rises. For the United States, see Lenore Weitzman, *The Divorce Revolution: The Unexpected Social and Economic Consequences for Women and Children in America* (New York: Free Press, 1985), 324–43. For England, see John Eekelaar and Mavis Maclean, *Maintenance after Divorce* (Oxford: Clarendon Press, 1986), 102 (maintenance paid by fathers was less than 10 percent of their own household income in two-thirds of the cases in the small sample studied). See also David Chambers, *Making Fathers Pay: The Enforcement of Child Support* (Chicago: University of Chicago Press, 1979), 42–58; Lenore Weitzman, "The Economics of Divorce: Social and Economic Consequences of Property, Alimony and Child Support Awards," 28 *U.C.L.A. Law Review* 1181, 1265–66 (1981); S. Hoffman and J. Holmes, "Husbands, Wives, and Divorce," in *Five Thousand American Families—Patterns of Economic Progress,* ed. G. Duncan and J. Morgan (Ann Arbor, Mich.: Institute for Social Research, 1976), IV, 23–75; Robert E. McGraw, Gloria J. Sterin, and Joseph M. Davis, "A Case Study in Divorce Law Reform and Its Aftermath," 20 *Journal of Family Law* 443 (1981–82).

68. Kamerman and Kahn, *Income Transfers,* 126, 307.

69. Blanche Bernstein, "Shouldn't Low-Income Fathers Support Their Families?" *The Public Interest* 55, 66 (1982).

70. Carol S. Bruch, "Developing Standards for Child Support Payments: A Critique of Current Practice," 16 *U.C.-Davis Law Review* 49 (1982).

71. For a detailed description of how the West German table-based system works in practice, see Philipp Wendl and Siegfried Staudigl, *Das Unterhaltsrecht in der familienrechtlichen Praxis* (Munich: Beck, 1986).

72. Child Support Enforcement Amendments of 1984, 42 U.S.C. Section 651.

73. Ibid., at Section 667(a).

74. Agell, "Social Security," 181.

75. Ibid.

76. Rune Lavin, *General Support of Families with Children in Swedish Welfare Law* (Report to 5th World Congress of the International Society on Family Law, July 1985, Brussels, Belgium) (forthcoming).

77. Alfred J. Kahn and Sheila B. Kamerman, "Social Assistance: An Eight Country Overview," 8 *Journal of the Institute for Socioeconomic Studies* 93, 102 (1983–84). See also Kamerman and Kahn, *Income Transfers,* 310.

78. Ibid., 126.

79. Committee on Ways and Means, U.S. House of Representatives, *Children in Poverty* (Washington: U.S. Government Printing Office, 1985), 196.

80. Lenore Weitzman, *The Divorce Revolution,* 341; McGraw, Sterin, and Davis, "A Case Study in Divorce Law Reform," 443; Joan Krauskopf, "Maintenance: A Decade of Development," 50 *Missouri Law Review* 259, 317 (1985).

81. "Divorce, Child Custody, and Child Support," in Bureau of the Census, U.S. Dept. of Commerce, *Current Population Reports, Special Studies* 8 (Series P-23, No. 84, 1979).

82. For example, Uniform Marriage and Divorce Act, 9A U.L.A. Section 308 (1973) and Comment.

83. Ibid., Prefatory Note, 9A U.L.A. 93, 160–61 (1973).

84. This argument draws on previous discussions of the "children-first" principle in Mary Ann Glendon, "Property Rights upon Dissolution of Marriages and Informal Unions," in *The Cambridge Lectures: 1981,* 245, 253 ff. (1983); *The New Family and the New Property,* 82; "Fixed Rules and Discretion in Contemporary Family Law and Succession Law," 60 *Tulane Law Review* 1165 (1986); "Family Law Reform in the 1980's," 44 *Louisiana Law Review* 1553, 1560 (1984).

85. See the summary of the property division laws of the fifty-one American jurisdictions in the "1985 Survey of American Family Law," 11 *Family Law Reporter* 3015, 3121 ff. (1985), and *Divorce: Equitable Distribution Doctrine,* 41 American Law Reports 4th 481 (1985) (hereafter A.L.R.). Three community property states (California, Louisiana, and New Mexico) follow an equal division rule, and a presumption favoring equal division of whatever property is subject to reallocation upon divorce exists in a minority of American jurisdictions. See "1985 Survey of American Family Law," 11 *Family Law Reporter* 3015, 3022–3026.

86. Mass. Gen. Laws Ch. 208 Sect. 34 (1985 Cum. Supp.): "Alimony or assignment of estate; determination of amount . . . Upon divorce or upon a complaint in an action brought at any time after a divorce . . . the court . . . may make a judgment for either of the parties to pay alimony to the other. In addition to or in lieu of a judgment to pay alimony, the court may assign to either husband or wife all or any part of the estate of the other. In determining the amount of alimony, if any, to be paid, or in fixing the nature and value of the property, if any, to be so assigned, the court, after hearing the witnesses, if any, of each party, shall consider the length of the marriage, the conduct of the parties during the marriage, the age, health, station, occupation, amount and sources of income, vocational skills, employability, estate, liabilities and needs of each of the parties and the opportunity of each for future acquisition of capital assets and income. The court may also consider the contribution of each of the parties in the acquisition, preservation or appreciation in value of their respective estates and the contribution of each of the parties as a homemaker to the family unit."

87. Harry D. Krause, *Child Support in America: The Legal Perspective* (Charlottesville, Va.: Michie, 1981), 3–18.

88. The idea is not a new one. No one has stated it more clearly than the Archbishop of Canterbury's Group: "The needs of any children of a marriage to be dissolved should as a rule be made first charge on all available assets, with the object of enabling them to be brought up with as nearly as possible the same standard of opportunity as they would have enjoyed had the marriage not failed. To that end, it would in some circumstances be necessary to award a spouse, *qua* guardian of children, a level of maintenance that would not otherwise be due; for provision for children should always include suitable provision for the person given the care of them." *Putting Asunder,* 73–74. Other writers who contend that the law should distinguish between the economic effects of divorces involving children and other divorces are John Eekelaar and Mavis Maclean, *Maintenance after Divorce* (Oxford: Clarendon Press, 1986), 141–49.

89. See "Divorce and Separation: Effect of Trial Court Giving Consideration to Needs of Children," 19 A.L.R. 4th 239 (1983).

90. Under federal income tax law, "alimony" is deductible by the payor-spouse and taxable to the recipient (Internal Revenue Code, Sections 71 and 215). Child support is neither deductible by the payor nor taxable to the payee. When the payor-spouse earns significantly more than the recipient, the tax consequences for both are usually minimized (and more income made available for both) by designating the payments as alimony. Prior to 1984, the issue of whether the parties' own characterization of payments would be accepted for tax purposes was determined under state law. The domestic relations tax provisions of the Deficit Reduction Act of 1984 (Publ. L. No. 98-367, 98 Stat. 494, 1984) have now established a federal standard for determining what types of payments will qualify as alimony and what will be considered child support. Within broad limits, however, the parties are still given substantial freedom to allocate the tax consequences of periodic payments. Stanley Surrey, William Warren, Paul McDaniel and Hugh Ault, *Federal Income Taxation—1985 Supplement,* I, 421–23. Thus it is to be expected that the practice of characterizing such payments, where possible, as alimony will continue to be typical in the commonly occurring situation where the noncustodial parent earns more than the custodian.

91. Robert H. Mnookin and Lewis Kornhauser, "Bargaining in the Shadow of the Law: The Case of Divorce," 88 *Yale Law Journal* 950, 951 n. 3 (1979).

92. Gwynn David, Alison MacLeod and Mervyn Murch, "Divorce: Who Supports the Family?" 13 *Family Law* 217, 223 (1983).

93. Edward M. Ginsburg, *Family Law Guidebook: A Handbook with Forms* (Stoneham, Mass.: Butterworths, 1984), 159.

94. Matrimonial and Family Proceedings Act 1984, Section 25(1).

95. There is much evidence that mothers readily cease pressing financial claims when threatened with litigation over custody, even when their lawyers can give them a high degree of assurance of ultimate success. See Phyllis Chesler,

Mothers on Trial: A Battle for Children and Custody (New York: McGraw Hill, 1985); Howard Erlanger, Elizabeth Chambliss, and Marygold Melli, *Coopera-tion or Coercion? Informal Settlement in the Divorce Context* (University of Wisconsin Institute for Legal Studies, Disputes Processing Research Program, Working Paper 7-6, March 1986), 22.

96. Richard Neely, *The Divorce Decision: The Legal and Human Conse-quences of Ending a Marriage* (New York: McGraw-Hill, 1984), 62.

97. Ibid.

98. Ibid., 62, 66. See also Mnookin and Kornhauser, "Bargaining in the Shadow of the Law," 950, 972–73 n. 77 (1979): "The prevailing best interests standard exacerbates the disadvantages of a risk-averse parent because of its great uncertainty."

99. Lenore J. Weitzman and Ruth B. Dixon, "Child Custody Awards: Legal Standards and Empirical Patterns for Child Custody, Support and Visita-tion After Divorce," 12 *U.C.-Davis Law Review* 471, 490 (1979).

100. See generally, Joseph Goldstein, Anna Freud, and Alfred Solnit, *Be-yond the Best Interests of the Child* (New York: Free Press, 1973); Robert J. Burt, "Experts, Custody Disputes and Legal Fantasies," 14 *Psychiatric Hospital* 140 (1983); David L. Chambers, "Rethinking the Substantive Rules for Custody Disputes in Divorce," 83 *Michigan Law Review* 477 (1984).

101. Burt, "Experts," 141–42.

102. *Garska v. McCoy*, 278 S.E. 2d 357 (W. Va. 1981). See also, R. Neely, *The Divorce Decision*, 79–83.

103. Ibid., 83. David Chambers has recently argued in favor of a legal preference for the primary caretaker of children aged five and under in custody disputes. Chambers, however, thinks the other parent should be allowed to rebut the presumption either by clear and convincing evidence or perhaps just a pre-ponderance of the evidence rather than having to show the primary caretaker is unfit. Chambers, "Rethinking," at 561–63.

104. See generally, Jeff Atkinson, "Criteria for Deciding Child Custody in the Trial and Appellate Courts," 18 *Family Law Quarterly* 1, 16–19 (1984); *Primary Caretaker Role of Respective Parents as Factor in Awarding Custody of Child,* 41 A.L.R. 4th 1129 (1985). Under guidelines worked out by a joint committee of the Massachusetts Bar Association and the Massachusetts Psychiat-ric Society, children under the age of four in that state are supposed to be placed "with the person who has been primarily responsible for their rearing." E. Gins-burg, *Family Law Guidebook,* 171.

105. For example, Cal. Civ. Code Ann. Tit. 3, Sect. 4550 ff.; Florida Rule of Civil Procedure 1.611 (reported in 10 *Family Law Reporter* 148, 1984); Nevada Rev. Stat. Ch. 125.181–125.184; Ore. Rev. Stat. Ch. 107, Sect. 107.485. The Oregon and California statutes make summary divorce available only to couples who have not accumulated substantial property and who have been married less than ten and five years, respectively.

106. In California, a court may make an offsetting award against the share

of a party who has "deliberately misappropriated" property to the exclusion of the interests of the other spouse. Cal. Civ. Code Sect. 4800.

107. Over fifty years ago Benjamin N. Cardozo urged the United States to follow the continental example in "A Ministry of Justice," 35 *Harvard Law Review* 113 (1921).

108. Law Commissions Act 1965 Section 3(1).

109. For a discussion of the type and extent of such influence, see Glendon, "Property Rights," 249.

110. M. Rheinstein, *Marriage Stability,* 406.

111. J. Commaille et al., "Le Divorce," 226.

112. In their interviews with a wide cross-section of Americans, Robert Bellah and his co-authors found that most people they talked to "used a language influenced by therapy to articulate their thoughts about interpersonal relationships." Robert Bellah et al., *Habits of the Heart: Individualism and Commitment in American Life* (Berkeley: University of California Press, 1985), 138.

113. Ibid., 129.

114. For a wealth of illustrations of how the evolving case law in fault divorces defines and redefines the obligations of marriage in France, see Françoise Dekeuwer-Defossez, "Impressions de recherche sur les fautes causes de divorce," *Recueil Dalloz,* Chr. 219–26 (1985).

115. West German *Bürgerliches Gesetzbuch* Section 1353.

116. David Chambers, "The Coming Curtailment of Compulsory Child Support," 80 *Michigan Law Review* 1614–15 (1982).

117. Ibid., 1614.

118. Ibid., 1623.

119. Ibid., 1625.

120. Ibid., 1634.

121. Ibid., 1614.

122. See Chambers, *Making Fathers Pay.*

3. Why the American Difference?

1. Robert Bellah, Richard Macken, William Sullivan, Ann Swidler and Steven Tipton, *Habits of the Heart: Individualism and Commitment in American Life* (Berkeley: University of California Press, 1985), 6.

2. Ibid., 20–21.

3. Thomas L. Pangle, *The Laws of Plato: Translated with Notes and an Interpretive Essay* (New York: Basic Books, 1980), 94.

4. Montesquieu described England as a nation "passionately fond of its liberty," where "every individual is independent," and where "each considers himself a monarch; and, indeed, the men . . . are rather confederates than fellow-subjects." *The Spirit of the Laws,* chap. 19, trans. Thomas Nugent (New York: Hafner, 1949). The English, he said, "know better than any other people upon

earth how to value, at the same time, these three great advantages—religion, commerce, and liberty" (ibid., chap. 20). Max Weber relied heavily on English and American examples to illustrate his thesis in *The Protestant Ethic and the Spirit of Capitalism,* trans. Talcott Parsons (London: G. Allen & Unwin, 1948). See also C. B. Macpherson, *The Political Theory of Possessive Individualism: Hobbes to Locke* (Oxford: Clarendon Press, 1962), and Marc Bloch, "A Contribution Towards a Comparative History of European Societies," in *Land and Work in Mediaeval Europe: Selected Papers* 44–81, trans. J. E. Anderson (London: Routledge and Kegan Paul, 1967).

5. Alexis de Tocqueville, *The Old Regime and the French Revolution,* trans. Stuart Gilbert (Garden City, N.Y.: Doubleday Anchor, 1955), 96 (first published 1856).

6. Marcel Waline, *L'Individualisme et le droit* (Paris: Domat Montchrestien, 1945), 323.

7. William H. McNeill, *History of Western Civilization,* rev. and enl. ed. (Chicago: University of Chicago Press, 1969), 533.

8. From 1804 to 1970 article 213 of the *Code Civil* stated: "Le mari est le chef de la famille." Until 1985 article 1421 declared: "Le mari administre seul les biens de la communauté."

9. Alan Macfarlane, *The Origins of English Individualism: The Family, Property and Social Transition* (Oxford: Basil Blackwell, 1979), 165–66.

10. Alasdair C. MacIntyre, *After Virtue: A Study in Moral Theory* (Notre Dame, Ind.: University of Notre Dame Press, 1981), 36.

11. See Michael G. Kammen, *People of Paradox: An Inquiry Concerning the Origins of American Civilization* (New York: Alfred A. Knopf, 1972), 58, 113–15.

12. R. Jackson Wilson, *In Quest of Community: Social Philosophy in the United States 1860–1920* (New York: Wiley and Sons, 1968), 1. See also Lawrence M. Friedman, *A History of American Law,* 2d ed. (New York: Simon and Schuster, 1985), 114.

13. Ibid., 21.

14. Alexis de Tocqueville, *Democracy in America,* trans. J. Mayer (Garden City, N.Y.: Doubleday Anchor, 1969), II, 536.

15. Ibid., 537.

16. Ibid., 513.

17. Tocqueville, *Democracy in America,* I, 69–70.

18. Ibid., 70.

19. Ibid., II, 590.

20. *United Nations Demographic Yearbook 1968* (New York: United Nations, 1968), Table 34.

21. R. Bellah, et al., *Habits of the Heart:* "Whereas a community attempts to be an inclusive whole, celebrating the interdependence of public and private life and of the different callings of all, lifestyle is fundamentally segmental and celebrates the narcissism of similarity. It usually explicitly involves a contrast

with others who 'do not share one's lifestyle'. For this reason, we speak not of lifestyle communities, but of lifestyle enclaves" (72).

22. For example, Marc Bloch, *Feudal Society*, trans. L. A. Manyon (Chicago: University of Chicago Press, 1961), 262.

23. Tocqueville, *Democracy in America*, II, 314. See also Hannah Arendt's conclusion in *The Origins of Totalitarianism* (San Diego: Harcourt Brace Jovanovich, 1973), 478: "What prepares men for totalitarian domination in the non-totalitarian world is the fact that loneliness, once a borderline experience usually suffered in certain marginal social conditions like old age, has become an everyday experience of the evergrowing masses of our century. The merciless process into which totalitarianism drives and organizes the masses looks like a suicidal escape from this reality. The 'ice cold reasoning' and the 'mighty tentacle' of dialectics which 'seizes you as in a vise' appears like a last support in a world where nobody is reliable and nothing can be relied upon."

24. Sir Edward Coke, *The First Part of the Institutes of the Lawes of England*, 97b.

25. Thomas Hobbes, *Leviathan* (London: Dent Dutton, 1973), chap. 26 (first published 1651).

26. W. Blackstone, *Commentaries on the Laws of England*, Book I, 17. Blackstone acknowledged parliamentary sovereignty in no uncertain terms: "It hath sovereign and uncontrollable authority in making, confirming, enlarging, restraining, abrogating, repealing, reviving and expounding of laws, concerning matters of all possible denominations, ecclesiastical or temporal, civil, military, maritime, or criminal: this being the place where that absolute despotic power, which must in all governments reside somewhere, is entrusted by the constitution of these kingdoms . . . It can, in short, do everything that is not naturally impossible; and therefore some have not scrupled to call its power, by a figure rather too bold, the omnipotence of parliament. True it is, that what the parliament doth, no authority upon earth can undo . . . So long, therefore, as the English constitution lasts, we may venture to affirm, that the power of parliament is absolute and without control." Ibid., 160–62. See also ibid., 91: "But if the parliament will positively enact a thing to be done which is unreasonable, I know of no power in the ordinary forms of the constitution that is vested with authority to control it." Having said all this, however, Blackstone devoted relatively little of his great treatise to discussing the output of the legislative branch.

27. Albert Vann Dicey, *Lectures on the Relation Between Law and Public Opinion in England During the 19th Century*, 2d ed. (London: Macmillan, 1952), 183 (first published 1905). On Mill's influence generally, see pp. 386, 428, 431–32.

28. John Stuart Mill, "On Liberty," in *Utilitarianism, Liberty and Representative Government* (New York: Dutton, 1951), 85, 95–96 (first published 1859). Cf. French Declaration of the Rights of Man and of the Citizen of August 26, 1789, Arts. IV and V: "Liberty consists in being able to do anything which does not injure another: therefore, the exercise of the natural rights of each man

has no limits other than those which assure to the other members of society the enjoyment of these same rights. These limits may be determined only by the law. V. The law may prohibit only those actions which are harmful to society. What is not prohibited by the law may not be prevented; and no one may be compelled to do what is not required by law." Henry deVries and Nina Galston, *Materials for the French Legal System* (New York: Parker School, 1969), 4.

29. John Stuart Mill, "On Liberty," 95, 215.

30. Ibid., 219–20.

31. Ibid., 216.

32. 434 U.S. 374 (1978).

33. John Stuart Mill, "On Liberty," 220.

34. Ibid.

35. Ibid., 213–14.

36. Francis Biddle, *Mr. Justice Holmes* (New York: Charles Scribner's Sons, 1942), 33.

37. No one has described the process better than Edward H. Levi, *An Introduction to Legal Reasoning* (Chicago: University of Chicago Press, 1948), 1–27.

38. Tort law (which is still essentially judge-made) remains, to an exceptional degree, an area of American law where individual responsibility is stressed along with individual rights and where the law continues to provide "a grassroots response to the injuries typical of our complex society," and to function both as "a mirror of morals and a legal vehicle for helping to define them." Special Committee on the Tort Liability System, *Towards a Jurisprudence of Injury: The Continuing Creation of a System of Substantive Justice in American Tort Law,* Marshall S. Shapo, Reporter (Chicago: American Bar Association, 1984), 12–1, 12–5.

39. See Mary Ann Glendon, "The Sources of Law in a Changing Legal Order," 17 *Creighton Law Review* 663, 673–77 (1983–1984).

40. James W. Miller, *Rousseau: Dreamer of Democracy* (New Haven: Yale University Press, 1984), 139.

41. Ibid., 145.

42. See, generally, Mary Ann Glendon, Michael W. Gordon, and Christopher Osakwe, *Comparative Legal Traditions* (St. Paul: West Publishing, 1985), 40–47.

43. Jean Carbonnier, "La Passion des lois au siècle des lumières," in his *Essais sur les lois* (Paris: Defrénois, 1979), 205.

44. Ibid., 203.

45. W. Blackstone, *Commentaries on the Laws of England,* Book I, 69.

46. Robert A. Ferguson, *Law and Letters in American Culture* (Cambridge: Harvard University Press, 1984), 14.

47. Jean-Jacques Rousseau, *The Social Contract and Discourses,* trans. G. D. H. Cole (London: Dent Dutton, 1973), 194.

48. Ibid., 124.

49. Leo Strauss, *Natural Right and History* (Chicago: University of Chicago Press, 1953), 287.

50. R. Ferguson, *Law and Letters:* "All of our formative documents—the Declaration of Independence, the Constitution, the Federalist Papers, and the seminal decisions of the Supreme Court under John Marshall—were drafted by attorneys steeped in Sir William Blackstone's *Commentaries on the Laws of England* (1765–1769)" (11). According to Daniel Boorstin, "In the first century of American independence, the *Commentaries* were not merely an approach to the study of law; for most lawyers they constituted all there was of the law." Daniel J. Boorstin, *The Mysterious Science of the Law* (Cambridge: Harvard University Press, 1941), 3. See also Lawrence M. Friedman, *A History of American Law,* 2d ed. (New York: Simon and Schuster, 1985), 109, 112.

51. *The Federalist Papers,* No. 37 (James Madison) (New York: Mentor, 1961).

52. John P. Dawson, *The Oracles of the Law* (Ann Arbor: University of Michigan Law School, 1968), 380.

53. Donald R. Kelley, *Historians and the Law in Postrevolutionary France* (Princeton: Princeton University Press, 1984), 53.

54. Ibid.

55. J. Carbonnier, "Tendances actuelles de l'art législatif en France," in *Essais sur les lois,* 231, 238.

56. J.-J. Rousseau, *The Social Contract,* 197.

57. Declaration of the Rights of Man and of the Citizen of August 26, 1789, in H. deVries and N. Galston, *Materials for the French Legal System,* 3–4.

58. French Civil Code, Art. 544. See also German Civil Code Sect. 903: "The owner of a thing may, to the extent that it is not contrary to the law or the rights of third parties, deal with the thing as he pleases and exclude others from any interference."

59. W. Blackstone, *Commentaries on the Laws of England,* Book II, 2.

60. French Civil Code, Art. 1134.

61. See, generally, Clyde W. Summers, "Individual Protection Against Unjust Dismissal: Time for a Statute," 62 *Virginia Law Review* 481, 508–19 (1976).

62. See, generally, John P. Dawson, *Gifts and Promises* (New Haven: Yale University Press, 1980).

63. See F. J. M. Feldbrugge, "Good and Bad Samaritans: A Comparative Survey of Criminal Law Provisions Concerning Failure to Rescue," 14 *American Journal of Comparative Law* 630 (1966); Marshall S. Shapo, *The Duty to Act: Tort Law, Power, and Public Policy* (Austin, Texas: University of Texas Press, 1977); Ernest J. Weinrib, "The Case for a Duty to Rescue," 90 *Yale Law Journal* 247 (1980).

64. Federal Constitutional Court decision of July 7, 1970, translated in Donald P. Kommers, "Liberty and Community in Constitutional Law: The

Abortion Cases in Comparative Perspective," 1985 *Brigham Young University Law Review* 371, 403.

65. See Bruce C. Hafen, "The Constitutional Status of Marriage, Kinship, and Sexual Privacy—Balancing the Individual and Social Interests," 81 *Michigan Law Review* 463 (1983).

66. H. deVries and N. Galston, *Materials for the French Legal System,* 6.

67. Ibid., 3.

68. Daniel S. Lev, *Colonial Law and the Genesis of the Indonesian State* (forthcoming).

69. Daniel Patrick Moynihan, *Family and Nation* (San Diego: Harcourt Brace Jovanovich, 1986); Alva Myrdal, *Nation and Family: The Swedish Experiment in Democratic Family and Population Policy* (Cambridge, Mass.: M.I.T. Press, 1968).

70. Decree No. 82-938 of 28 October 1982, creating a medal of the French family, *Journal officiel,* November 4, 1982, 3314. It is to be noted that unlike the Soviet Union, which awards medals for the *bearing* of numerous children, France rewards the *raising* of children in such a way as to be an example to the community.

71. For a history and assessment of the current status of the welfare state on the continent see François Ewald, *L'Etat providence* (Paris: Grasset, 1986).

72. Samuel H. Preston, "Children and the Elderly in the U.S.," 251–6 *Scientific American* 44–49 (December 1984).

73. D. Moynihan, *Family and Nation,* 5.

74. Tocqueville, *Democracy in America,* I, 51–54.

75. Ibid., II, 508.

76. Ibid., 548.

77. Ibid., 549.

78. For dozens of examples of how the United States Constitution is simultaneously revered and misunderstood, see Michael Kammen, *A Machine That Would Go of Itself: The Constitution in American Culture* (New York: Knopf, 1986).

79. They have, for example attracted such constitutional law scholars as Michael Perry and Laurence Tribe. See Chapter 1, above. More than any other legal writer, James B. White has worked out and illustrated a theory of law as constitutive conversation in a series of beautifully written essays. See his *When Words Lose Their Meaning: Constitutions and Reconstitutions of Language, Character, and Community* (Chicago: University of Chicago Press, 1984); and *Heracles' Bow: Essay on the Rhetoric and Poetics of Law* (Madison, Wis.: University of Wisconsin, 1985).

80. Jürgen Habermas, *The Theory of Communicative Action: Reason and the Rationalization of Society,* trans. T. McCarthy (Boston: Beacon Press, 1984), I; A. MacIntyre, *After Virtue,* 207.

81. Ibid., 206.

82. Tocqueville, *Democracy in America*, I, 287.

83. A. MacIntyre, *After Virtue*, 245.

84. R. Bellah et al., *Habits of the Heart*, 20.

85. Clifford Geertz, *Local Knowledge: Further Essays in Interpretive Anthropology* (New York: Basic Books, 1983), 175.

86. Plato, *The Laws*, 969 (trans. T. Pangle).

87. Plato, *Phaedo*, 78ª; *The Laws*, 951.

88. See Plato, *Phaedo*, 78ª.

INDEX